An Introduction to Safe Driving

A Guide for the Women of the Kingdom of Saudi Arabia and Their Families

By Phil Berardelli

Security Management International
Vienna, Virginia

An Introduction to Safe Driving
A Guide for the Women of Saudi Arabia and Their Families

© 2018 Security Management International – All Rights Reserved

Published in the United States of America

ISBN 978-1-7324297-4-1

Cover Photo Credit: IStock.com/Swisshippo

Design by Camille Mouillard

Printed in the United States of America

No part of this book may be reproduced, stored in a data base or other retrieval system, or transmitted in any form by any means, including mechanical, electronic, photo-copying, recording or otherwise, without the prior written permission of the publisher.

Foreword

Dear Ladies: Greetings from America!

Recently, Princess Reema bint Bandar Al Saud granted an interview to an American television program called "60 Minutes" and mentioned that your government is planning to teach many thousands of Saudi women to drive. When I learned about the decision, I wrote to Princess Reema and offered this book as an aid to the process. I want to help you, the women of Saudi Arabia, become safe and competent drivers, and I hope the information in this book will serve you well throughout your lifetime behind the wheel.

I am a journalist and author who has been writing about driving safety for many years. I began covering the topic nearly three decades ago in a newspaper article, in which I described my efforts to teach my two daughters how to drive. In the years since, I have written many articles on safe driving as well as three books – the first for young people, the second for individuals called "aggressive drivers" in an attempt to help them curb their dangerous behavior, and the third for elderly people to help them to continue to drive safely. Now, I would like to offer to you the knowledge and experience I have accumulated.

I have based this new book on my previous writings, but I have also changed some of the instructional guidelines to reflect the improved technology featured in the types of vehicles you will be operating. And I have tried to adapt the text to conform to your country's laws, requirements and other relevant factors.

I hope you will find this material easy to follow and easy to remember. Above all, I hope it will help you gain the confidence and skills you will need to join the driving population of your country in a safe and comfortable manner.

With my best wishes,
Phil Berardelli

TABLE OF CONTENTS

HOW TO USE THIS BOOK 1

INTRODUCTION FOR THE STUDENT 4

INTRODUCTION FOR THE INSTRUCTOR 6

TEN STEPS TO BASIC SKILLS...12

STEP ONE: Basic Moves 13
STEP TWO: Quiet Streets, Back Roads.......................................19
STEP THREE: Busy But Slow Encounters....................................28
STEP FOUR: Stop and Go 31
STEP FIVE: Countryside..42
STEP SIX: Getting Up to Highway Speeds 59
STEP SEVEN: Night Driving...73
STEP EIGHT: City Streets..76
STEP NINE: Into Heavy Traffic 80
STEP TEN: Harsh Weather 91

TWO LAST ITEMS 103

GO FORTH WITH PRIDE AND CONFIDENCE..............................104

LESSON GUIDE 105

LESSON LOG 111

HOW TO USE THIS BOOK

[For the Student and the Instructor]

In this age of the Internet, laptop computers, digital readers and smartphones, books seem to occupy a less important role in our daily lives. But sometimes books can be useful, and driving instruction is one such time. Yes, you could be reading these words digitally, but I recommend that you consider using the printed version, which I hope you will keep with you in the vehicle while you proceed with the lessons.

"In the vehicle" is the key phrase, because I believe the best place to learn how to drive is on the road, not in front of a video screen or computer monitor. Good skills and road sense develop only through repeated and lengthy exposure to real situations and sensations. This is true even for the most sophisticated simulators. Although they can provide an approximation of the experience of driving, they do so imperfectly and without consequence – although I agree they offer a higher degree of safety.

I also recommend that you, the instructor, and you, the student, read this book completely before beginning the lessons. If you do, you will notice that I have written certain sections of the book for the student and crafted other passages for the instructor. There is also a crossover. You, the student, cannot use the book while driving, so you should study the relevant sections ahead of time while you, the instructor, should help the student recall those sections during the lessons.

I have divided the lessons into 10 steps, but each step contains much to remember. You both should refer to the book often. There is an effective way to do this. Here is how it works:
 - Before beginning a driving session, each of you should read the relevant text.
 - During the lesson, the instructor should refer to the text as necessary to make sure the student covers all of the material and performs the exercises correctly and well.
 - After the lesson, both of you should spend a few minutes discussing how the session went. Did the student understand everything? What went well? Were there difficulties?

I have included a Lesson Log in the printed version of the book to help you record the results of the individual sessions. If you are using the digital version, perhaps you can bring along a small notebook for the same purpose or create a file for your notes on your mobile device. Whatever method you choose, try to keep track of your progress and of any problems that appear and require special attention.

When you have completed all of the lessons, keep the book for quick reference whenever necessary – perhaps store it in the glove compartment – because you might find it useful from time to time.

TEN STEPS AND FIVE THEMES

This book is about acquiring driving skills, but it is also about learning and maintaining a good driving attitude. In fact, as I will describe later, a good attitude can be even more important than good skills.

This is true particularly during the early driving years, when those skills are still developing. Inexperience can be dangerous on the roads of any country, but good attitude can compensate somewhat for the lack of skills. That is why, in addition to 10 steps, I have furnished five basic themes – approaches – to driving that the student should learn. I will introduce them at appropriate times, and they appear at various places in the text. The five themes are:

- CLEAR THE WAY
- LEARN THE LIMITS
- SHARE THE ROAD
- THINK AHEAD
- FEEL THE ROAD

The themes represent important safety information. As the specifics of the individual lessons fade into the past, I hope the themes will linger in your memory. Such thoughts were uppermost in my mind when I taught my own children to drive. Unlike my youth, when a friend and I learned the basics in an ancient vehicle called a Studebaker, as we bumped safely across empty fields and over little-traveled dirt roads in rural America, you two will likely teach and practice driving in a densely populated area, where main arteries are multi-laned highways with high speed limits.

Despite the greater challenges facing you both, I believe this book will assist you effectively. It is structured to help anyone willing to take on the task of instruction. It is a common-sense approach, intended to provide the basic information you need to turn your student into a competent beginning driver.

As you, the student, will quickly see, this book takes a developmental, step-by-step approach. You begin simply and proceed carefully through increasingly complex tasks. With the help of your instructor, you master each set of skills before moving on. You, the instructor, do not need the expertise of a race-car driver to provide a firm foundation. Even at highway speeds, the skills described herein can keep you both safe – if the student practices them consistently and you give her the time to develop.

Time is the critical factor. How much time? A lot – though I will leave it to you both to decide. Indeed, there are many ways to approach this task effectively. It need not be overwhelming. You can tailor the instruction to fit your schedules. In whatever ways you can manage, however, I urge you, the student, to absorb the lessons. Habits take time to appear. This is something you should not hurry, and some of the instruction can even continue after you obtain the driver's license.

Yes, there are aspects of driving that should not be attempted too early. You should acquire and perfect your basic skills before undertaking the more complex – and potentially dangerous – tasks.

Go one step at a time. Do what you can when you can. If you have an hour or so each day to devote to lessons, then set aside that time and work every day. If you can work on this only two or three times a week, that can be a valid approach as well. At this writing, your government is still formulating how to accomplish the worthy goal of training tens of thousands of you ladies to join your country's population of motorists. But whatever path is chosen, the concepts and lessons I have set forth will help you in important ways.

Please study them seriously. Learn them well. Always drive safely.

INTRODUCTION FOR THE STUDENT

Good driving requires good skills.
More than that, good driving requires a good attitude.

Many things in life are your own business – your private thoughts and personal conversations, for examples. Driving is different. It is something you do on public roads, sharing space with many other people. What they do affects you, and what you do affects them. You want to be a model of good behavior and the right attitude.

Have you ever experienced mastering a new skill? Say, for example, you want to learn to prepare a meal. You might read some recipes and even memorize them. You watch a skilled chef on TV. But until you actually stand in a kitchen, with ingredients and utensils spread before you and begin the process of putting it all together by yourself, you cannot truly learn to cook.

It is important, therefore, to recognize that no matter how much time you spend in class using a driving simulator, or how many people explain driving to you, the biggest step you take is getting behind the wheel of a vehicle and expecting to move it in a proper and safe manner.

As you think about yourself as a woman doing this for the first time, try not to be apprehensive. Allow yourself time to master this new skill. You will have help.

First, you will have an instructor sitting right beside you. This will be someone you know and trust – a family member most likely. This person will want you to succeed and will provide support through the many hours required. Trust your instructor; let yourself be guided in this new endeavor.

Second, you will make mistakes. They are part of the process – they will help you to learn. Most people remember their mistakes and strive not to repeat them. That is precisely why the book's lessons begin with basic tasks conducted in empty areas – so the mistakes cannot bring harm to yourself or anyone else.

I do not want to belabor this point, but I must assert it. Driving should always be conducted with the utmost commitment to safety. I know this because I have experienced, several times, moments in which I behaved unsafely. As a result, I created situations of danger that arose with frightening suddenness and required me to react instantly to prevent a likely fatal crash. I fervently hope the instruction I have provided here will spare you from ever sharing similar moments.

For now, however, as you slide behind the wheel to begin this new phase of your life – that of a driver – please concentrate on the things that will make you feel confident.

For example, simply take a moment to enjoy how the world appears through the driver's side of the windshield. More practically, adjust the mirrors and seat to your comfort. Don't forget to buckle your seatbelt. Relax!

Then, insert and turn the key or push the button to make the machine come alive. Sit for another moment and feel the power you have ignited. This can be somewhat scary but thrilling. You are about to tame and move this large beast. Although you have never done this before, you can and ultimately will do well.

Along with mental ability, good driving takes a certain amount of physical strength and coordination. You probably will need to develop new motor skills. But what you as a woman at first might lack in the experience of handling large equipment you can offset with knowledge, alertness and competence.

Women can be excellent drivers. Indeed, in America and elsewhere women have compiled superior safety records on the highways. Women are patient and not likely to drive as competitively as some men do. And a woman's calm and caring nature allows her to focus on potential passengers: her children, older parents and friends. We call such passengers our precious cargo. I believe you will do the same, and your safe-driving skills can make a great contribution to your family. Such considerations will help you to form that good driving attitude I mentioned.

Something else to remember: Driving is exciting and fun – and a rewarding part of life.

So please, consider carefully the material and lessons in this book. Be patient and accept the guidance of your instructor. Develop good driving habits, because they will never let you down. Good skills and attitude will help you travel to your destinations safely and enjoyably. They will help you avoid harm to yourself, to loved ones and to anyone else you encounter on the road.

That is a goal worth striving for and achieving.

With encouragement, I say to you, the student:

- Be confident and begin slowly.
- Follow the rules.
- Practice, practice, practice.

INTRODUCTION FOR THE INSTRUCTOR

You might not have imagined a day when you would be teaching a family member to drive – or predicted that such instruction would ever be needed. But now your country has decided to extend the same privilege to its women as every other nation on earth. And, as I have advocated for years in the United States, the best possible instructor in this process is a family member.

I hope you will come to regard your efforts as one of the most important gifts you can give to someone close to you. Proper training behind the wheel, in your country as in mine, equals safety. I cannot overstate this. The Kingdom of Saudi Arabia experiences one of the highest highway crash rates in the world. In contrast, despite the huge number of vehicles on America's roads, and despite our nearly singular conceit of allowing teenagers to drive, our crash rates are much lower.

Furthermore, this new path for your country presents a unique challenge. Unlike other nations, in which women have been driving for many decades, traffic on your highways is about to receive an entirely new mix of motorists. And those new motorists, in general, will begin operating large machines for the first time in their lives. This situation could produce many unfortunate encounters. What do to?

No matter how extensive the new driver-training program, it cannot provide sufficient preparation. I know this fact because I have witnessed it for decades in the United States. Therefore, I argue that the only sensible solution is for families to complete the training. If you have decided to take on the task, I commend and admire you, for who better to train a loved one in such an important endeavor than someone who is close to and caring about her?

AN APPROACH TO TEACHING

As you study the material in this book, and prepare to teach the student, please keep in mind that everyone learns best by doing. It is an approach based firmly on principles of human psychology and physiology. The mind and body can adapt to many conditions and activities; it is a survival mechanism. The key to successful adaptation is repeated exposure.

Driving, learned properly, becomes automatic, allowing the mind to relax without sacrificing attention. The only way it can be learned properly is by repetition. Of course, spend time discussing what to do, but do not overdo it.

When I was a teacher, I discovered that certain methods can interfere with the learning process. For example, many people tend to teach by asking open-ended questions or posing "fill-in-the-blank" situations:

"What should you never do if you are approaching the crest of a hill?"

Or, "The most important thing to do after you start the engine is _____."

Or, they simply spend too much time lecturing about proper technique while sitting still.

Try to avoid these methods. They are ineffective and tend to create tension between the instructor and the student. People naturally react negatively to someone lecturing to them. If you recall your own experiences, I am sure you will agree.

Instead, briefly and in a straightforward way, tell the student exactly what you want her to know and explain the reason for it. Ask once in a while if she understands everything you have mentioned. Otherwise, keep things moving. Let the student perform the lessons.

As you proceed, try to include as much real-time instruction as possible. Calmly and matter-of-factly comment on the performance as it happens. Also – and this is important – act as the student's co-pilot. Keep your own attention well ahead – and behind – on the road. There will be many situations and hazards the student will not anticipate until she is more experienced. For examples:

- Developing congestion ahead,
- Vehicles that could emerge from blind entranceways or parking spaces,
- Certain impatient drivers whom you know will be tailgating and lane-weaving around you,
- And potholes, because most novice drivers seem particularly oblivious to potholes. Teach the student to avoid them or encounter them as slowly as possible.

There will be no shortage of road hazards, so you must serve double duty as instructor and co-pilot. You will find the co-pilot role valuable. It is the best way to impart knowledge, judgment and experience. By narrating road conditions and pointing out potential hazards, you will help your student develop and strengthen her awareness.

If she is not performing something correctly, say so as soon as you notice it – but do it gently. Mistakes are part of the process, so there is no need to become emotional. You have to expect them. Be calm and review what happened immediately.

Speaking of which, as I mentioned earlier, it is a good idea to spend a brief time at the end of each session reviewing everything that was covered and anything unexpected that happened. Do it while the session remains fresh in both of your minds. If the student experiences a particular or persistent problem, note it in the lesson log for future reference.

Regarding the lessons, I designed them to increase the level of complexity gradually. Repeat each step until the student begins making her own corrections and performs well and consistently.

If not, it is a risk to you both to move into a more complicated situation.

Remember to be just as quick to praise good performance as you are in pointing out mistakes. Be encouraging. It is a way to build a new driver's confidence and maintain a cordial relationship between the two of you.

Also remember: You have amassed your own body of experience on the road. Try to make use of it whenever you can. If you disagree with one of my recommendations, replace it with your own – feel free to customize the lessons. Or, present both sides and explain why you think your way is better.

Of the 10 steps I have recommended, you might decide that one or more of them does not warrant inclusion. If so – though I urge you to consider each one carefully – you might want to skip it temporarily or even omit it based on your judgment of what will best serve your student. Though I am certain my methods will provide a solid basic level of skills, they are by no means the only ways to do things. This process should not be about the book teaching the student. The book is a starting place. The process should be about you teaching the student – and using everything you have learned to help protect her.

The Best Place to Start

When you and the student have completed the preliminaries, and the student has acquired proper documentation, it is time to let her take control of the vehicle. Where should you start?

If the government has created or designated certain locations for instruction, then obviously that is where you should conduct the beginning lessons. Otherwise, the best place is a big, unoccupied parking lot. Some examples:

- An office or municipal building after working hours
- A shopping mall early in the morning
- A school or university when out of session

Try to find a parking lot that features several rows of spaces, so you can move along repeating and continuous patterns.

Empty parking lots are ideal because they offer plenty of space as well as defined areas; they are forgiving of errors. The one I chose for my daughters was in a nearby neighborhood park. It was perfect: two paved areas split by a grassy median and connected at both ends. It even had speed bumps, which also can be useful. Most important, although the lot was relatively small, it was almost always empty during the time we used it. Find an empty parking lot, and you will be ready to begin the instruction.

The First Day

Drive to the designated practice lot and pull into a parking space. Try to use a space with either a concrete stop or a curb at the end, so there is a visual reference. Put the gearshift in "park" and engage the parking brake. Turn the engine off then switch places.

The Pre-Drive Checklist

You should go over this list every time you begin a lesson, until the student can perform all actions without prompting.

- Check the windshield. It should be clear of any debris such as dust and leaves, and it should be clean. If not, immediately show the student how to use the windshield washer.

- Adjust the seat. It should allow the driver's foot to rest comfortably on the gas pedal without stretching, but it needs to be of sufficient distance that the foot can be moved quickly from the gas to the brake – again, without stretching. It is important for the driver to sit at least 25 centimeters away from the steering wheel to prevent injury if the airbag deploys. If the seat has other adjustments, such as height, make sure it is elevated enough to allow good visibility over the dashboard and all around. A common mistake among many drivers is to keep the seat too low. If the seat back can be adjusted, make sure it is not tilted backward too much. That can cause strain to the neck and arm muscles over time.

- Adjust the head restraint. The back of the driver's head should hit it in the center and should not have to travel more than a couple of inches before making contact.

- Adjust the steering wheel, if possible, so it is comfortable. The best position is tilting slightly away from the vertical, and the wheel should be far enough away from the body that when gripped it draws the elbows away from the chest.

- Adjust the mirrors. All of the mirrors should be properly positioned to give the widest possible field of vision behind the vehicle. The center mirror should give an equal view to the right and left behind. The side mirrors should show just the slightest view of the edge of the vehicle. This is important, because the vehicle edge gives the new driver a frame of reference for other vehicles and objects. On the other hand, if too much of the vehicle shows in the mirror, the driver's field of vision is probably too narrow. That is dangerous, because it will widen the blind spots.

Blind spots are gaps in vision, whether straight ahead or via the mirrors. If blind spots are large enough, other vehicles can occupy them and be hidden from the driver.

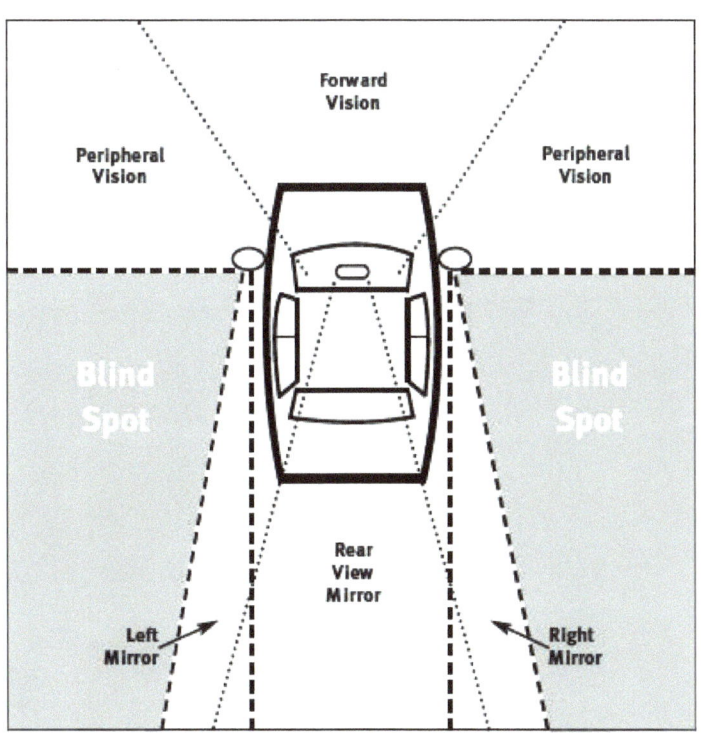

- Fasten the seatbelt. If the vehicle has an automatic belt, make sure it fits properly – and make sure you are belted also. Remind the student that all occupants should always fasten their belts.

- Lock the doors. This adds a measure of security. Most modern vehicles feature automatic locks that engage as soon as they begin moving forward. Locked doors are less likely to spring open in a crash, and they can prevent intruders – infrequent but real threats – from getting in.

Gripping the Wheel

The hand position on the steering wheel has become even more important since the introduction of airbags. Most experts recommend the "nine o'clock/three o'clock" position, to keep the hands away from the airbag in case it deploys during a crash. It also permits the rapid and easy movement of the wheel. In addition, I recommend either "ten o'clock/four o'clock," or "eight o'clock/two o'clock," depending on which feels more comfortable. Neither would interfere with the deployment of an airbag, and both offer plenty of control and flexibility, particularly if the hands are extended far enough away from the body. The position to stay away from – in terms of both control and airbag safety – is with one or both hands at the top of the wheel. It is common among drivers, but it interferes with effective vehicle control, and it invites injury if the airbag deploys.

I will mention a useful practice exercise soon. But for now, please remember to teach proper hand positions from the beginning.

TEN STEPS TO BASIC SKILLS

[For the Instructor]

Back in the 1950s, the U.S. National Aeronautics and Space Administration began a program to train astronauts. The key component of the approach involved something called conditioning. Scientists and technicians developed tests and exercises designed to simulate as closely as possible the experiences and sensations the astronauts would encounter on their missions.

The more experiences the mission planners could simulate, the more confident and successful the astronauts would be. Their fears could be "adapted out," as the designers of the training program often said.

That was the hypothesis. For a while, it could only be a hypothesis, because no one actually had gone into space. Nevertheless, the scientists did their best to simulate the expected conditions, and much of their work was later validated by the reality of the missions.

You can apply the same approach to driving, which is an endeavor that at first can seem unnerving and possibly frightening to someone with no experience. It also can be dangerous, if a novice driver is confronted with a situation for which she is unprepared. No novice, regardless of how bright and coordinated she might be, can jump into a car and instantly display skill and assurance. For one thing, the task requires too many decisions, and making those decisions correctly and consistently cannot be done through intuition.

Good driving behavior is based on experience – on developing reflexes. That is why it is so important to take sufficient time to teach the student to drive. She must adapt to the new sensations of being behind the wheel and whatever else she will encounter.

To accomplish this goal, we will cover 10 separate steps, each one more complex than the last. The idea is to begin slowly and simply and then move the student into more and more challenging conditions. For some students, the early material might seem too simple. It is not. It is fundamental. The early lessons will provide the foundation for the more complex tasks. Please, do not neglect them.

It is inadvisable to complete a step in one session. Cover as much as you can, and then begin the next session where you left off. The point is to make sure the student continues to practice a lesson task until she has mastered it. This is true particularly in the later stages, where the instruction takes place in traffic. Do not put the student in that situation until you are sure she can handle it. To do otherwise is dangerous.

STEP ONE: Basic Moves

[For the Instructor]

This lesson takes place in the empty parking lot and covers the simplest movement and steering of the vehicle. Each session in Step One should begin with the student driver repeating all of the points discussed in the previous section, plus one new item:

- Checking or cleaning the windshield
- Adjusting the seat and head restraint
- Adjusting the steering wheel
- Adjusting the mirrors
- Fastening the seatbelt
- Locking the doors
- Mentally clearing the zone around the vehicle

These steps might seem too simple, because you will only be inching around an empty parking lot. But remember, you are trying to teach good habits, so the student should become accustomed to performing basic tasks – or checking for them – every time she gets behind the wheel. Soon it will become automatic, a routine experience that will include certain specific sensations of adjustment and comfort: position of the mirrors, angle of the back, distance to the steering wheel and so on. At that point, if something does not feel right, the student will correct it. For now, have the student become accustomed to sitting properly in the driver's seat and making sure everything is in its preferred position.

Theme One of Five: CLEAR THE WAY

[For the Student]

As mentioned, the lessons in this book include the development of five main themes. They constitute five approaches to driving that underlie everything else there is to learn. We will cover the other four later. The first of the five is:

CLEAR THE WAY

It means never move the vehicle anywhere until you look first. You must constantly "clear" the way ahead or behind by looking, and you must stop or slow down whenever your ability to see where you are going is restricted. You should practice this from the very beginning and never forget it.

When you pull out of a parking space, make sure there is nothing immediately in front of or behind the vehicle. You can begin by looking around before you get in. Make a quick mental note. Are there any small children nearby? If so, might they wander in your path – particularly if you are backing up the vehicle – while you are getting ready to move? Are there toys or bicycles or shopping carts in the way? You want to clear an imaginary zone around the vehicle. The same applies as long as you are driving. When you start out, scan in all directions. Be sure you are clear.

Many modern vehicles are equipped with rear-facing cameras. They represent a significant safety advance, but they do not operate perfectly. Use the cameras, but do not rely completely on them. Make sure you are aware of everything surrounding the vehicle that could be a hazard.

Whenever you arrive at a stop sign or an intersection, keep looking in every direction where there might be approaching traffic. All drivers soon learn that it takes only a second or two of inattention to produce an unwanted surprise.

We will discuss this theme frequently as we go through the lessons, but for now concentrate on the idea: **CLEAR THE WAY**

Clean and Clear
Speaking of clear, remember to keep your windshield clean. The same goes for side and rear windows. This might seem unimportant, but whenever you drive at night or in bad weather, in the glare of oncoming headlights, it is something that can be annoying if not taken care of. It can be

dangerous. You might not notice a thin accumulation of dirt or other substances during normal driving, but I assure you a dirty windshield can produce a lot of glare that can interfere with your vision at night, particularly during rain or fog. So, please make sure your windshield is clean whenever you drive.

Patience, Patience

If all is ready, you can begin. For today, and as long as it seems proper to your instructor, you will be moving the vehicle slowly around the lot. And I mean s-l-o-w-l-y. The speed should be hardly more than the vehicle moves on its own.

- Turn the engine on.
- With the foot on the brake pedal, release the parking brake and move the gearshift into "reverse."

Do not move yet. Hold the vehicle still, in gear, engine running, foot on the brake. It is a new experience, so allow yourself to become accustomed to the feel of it for a moment.

Then, after a quick look on both sides (**CLEAR THE WAY**), slide your left hand to the top of the wheel, drape your right arm across the top of the seat, and then turn and look out the back window.

If you see anyone nearby, sit still; wait until the immediate area is clear. Likewise, during Step One, anytime a vehicle or pedestrian approaches, stop. You do not want to be interacting with anyone or anything at this point.

All clear? Good. Gently ease off the brake pedal. Allow the vehicle to move backward about 6 meters, so it is completely out of the space. Then, just as gently, depress the brake and stop.

You should be looking out the back window the whole time, not at your rearview mirror. You do not want to try any turns right away; backing up is too new for that. Now, face forward, shift from reverse into drive and move the vehicle back into the parking space. Try to match the front end with the curb or the edge of the pavement.

It might seem strange, backing up the vehicle for your first move, but one of the most important things to learn right away is where your vehicle's extremities are – its front and back corners. You need to gain a sense of the space the vehicle occupies before you can move it around and into tight places.

By starting with a small reverse move, you learn how much of the vehicle is behind you. When you pull back into the space, you begin to learn where the front end is.

Positioning the Vehicle

[For the Instructor]

Make sure the student pulls all the way into the space. The idea is to develop a sense of where the front of the vehicle is. When the maneuver is completed, have the student put the transmission back into park, engage the parking brake and shut off the engine. Then, have her get out and look where the front end is in relation to the end of the space.

If she places the vehicle properly on the first try, fine, but repeat the drill nevertheless and perhaps several times. If the student is having some trouble, take more time to repeat the exercise, over and over if necessary, until she can consistently place the front of vehicle successfully inside the parking space.

Around and Around

Next, begin moving around the lot. Have the student back out of the space and continue across the traffic lane into the facing space. Next, have her get out and check the vehicle's position again. No turning while backing up just yet. Follow this by having her pull forward into the traffic lane, turning one way or the other but signaling before turning. Begin circling the lot. She should use the signal every time there is a turn, just for practice. Emphasize steady motion and staying within lane markers.

Circling the parking lot offers an excellent time to instill good hand positions on the steering wheel. Many American drivers display the bad habit of holding their hands too high while steering. This not only can be dangerous in an emergency, because the position interferes with the free and rapid movement of the arms, but it also requires drivers to sit too close to the wheel, meaning they can be badly injured if the airbag deploys in a collision.

If you notice that the student is exhibiting these tendencies, have her circle the parking lot but keep her hands off the wheel. For several cycles, have the student keep her hands in her hap – except to correct the vehicle's heading. If the exercise works properly, she will need to move her hands up to the wheel and back down frequently. By doing so, she will begin to hold the wheel in a lower and safer position.

This practice maneuver helps to teach another important habit: using the eyes to determine where the vehicle should be heading and using the hands to obey those commands.

Practice 'Called Stops'
As you proceed with repetitions, occasionally say "Stop." Whenever you do, no matter what is going on, train your student to bring the vehicle to a complete stop, immediately. Not a panic stop, however. You do not want the tires to screech – just a firm, smooth stop. No questions asked. No warnings, an immediate stop. The idea is to get the student accustomed to moving quickly from the gas pedal to the brake.

Mention ahead of time that you are going to do this. Explain what you expect her to do and why.

The called stop is your safety net. Use it regularly until you get into real traffic situations. Practice it at unexpected times until the student reacts to it quickly and reliably. Then it will be available for emergencies. The student will become conditioned to hearing it, and you can be reasonably confident she will react properly.

Proper Steering

[For the Student]

When you approach a turn, keep your hands in position but gradually shuttle the wheel, either to the right or to the left. Practice keeping your hands in position. This might seem awkward now, but it is something important to learn.

When you have completed the turn, let the wheel slip gently through your fingers as the vehicle straightens out, and then grasp the wheel gently to proceed.

One tip: Avoid looking at your hands or the wheel. Always look where you want to go, and your hands will begin to steer the vehicle in that direction reflexively.

Keep It Slow

[For the Instructor]

Do not allow the student to move the vehicle more than about 15 kilometers an hour, only a little above idling speed, for the duration of Step One. Occasionally, have the student stop in the lane then start up again. Work on stopping and starting smoothly, easing on and off the brake, and pressing gently on the gas.

Next, have the student try turning into a parking space from the lane. Be sure she signals first. Do not offer help the first time but note how well the student places the vehicle within the space markers. No need to step outside again. Both of you open the doors and look down. The vehicle should be in the center of the space and parallel to the lines.

Backing Well

[For the Student]

Back out of the space again, but this time turn into the lane while you are moving. When backing, you can put your left hand on top of the wheel and keep that hand on the wheel while turning. It is true that using two hands gives more control, but keeping the right hand on the wheel prevents your body from turning around far enough to see completely behind you. It restricts your vision. When you move very slowly, you need vision more than two hands, and you can stop immediately if necessary. Here are some tips for backing out well:

- Keep alert so you do not bump into anything
- Back far enough out of the space so your next move is easy
- End each turn with your front wheels pointed in the direction of your next move.
- Turn the wheel only when the car is not moving.

That second tip can keep you from developing a common bad habit. Many drivers do not back far enough out of parking spaces. As a result, they usually need several back-and-forth moves before they can pull away freely. This requires more time to vacate the space, which in crowded lots can aggravate drivers who are blocked from moving. But you can demonstrate your skill and thoughtfulness by backing out well and pulling away quickly.

Begin circling the parking lot again, and after a while try backing into a space:

- Pull past the space slightly and turn away from it. Remember that before you stop, turn the wheels toward the next direction you want to go.

- Back the vehicle into the space. Look out the rear window and use the rear of the vehicle to guide you into proper position. Straighten the wheels before you stop.

It could take more than a few tries, but eventually you will feel comfortable. You might want to get out after the first time to see where the rear of the vehicle ended up. It should line up with the back of the space, not hang over onto the sidewalk or the ground.
Why would you want to back into a space? Because sometimes, in a crowded lot, it is easier and safer to drive out of a space into a traffic lane than try to back out.

All Together

[For the Instructor]

Now, practice all of the components of Step One: starting and stopping smoothly, staying within traffic lanes, turning, pulling into and backing out of parking spaces, and remembering the pre-drive checklist every time a lesson begins.

Perform all of this, of course, in the empty lot. Continue the exercises until the student can complete them with some precision and confidence – but not necessarily with perfection. No need to overdo things at this early stage.

STEP TWO: Quiet Streets, Back Roads

[For the Instructor]

After the student feels comfortable performing the parking lot exercises, it is time to take her on the road, but in a small way. Find the least-traveled nearby group of side streets available. Also, in that vicinity, find a parking lot that is not empty but not busy. You will want to keep to a low speed because you do not want to interfere with or impede other drivers.

There are plenty of suitable streets in most neighborhoods. The idea is to find an area to practice with light residential traffic. You do not want to use a thoroughfare yet.

People tend to be more patient if a student driver is crawling around a neighborhood than if she is doing so on a busy street or road. They can recognize a novice driver, and they likely will give her leeway. Not so on the traffic arteries. There, short tempers are common. A slow-moving vehicle can be viewed as an invasion of territory. Stay away for now.

If the student can drive directly to your destination without encountering traffic, let her do so. If not, you drive. Find a quiet place to park then switch seats. Again, start each session with the pre-drive checklist.

Continue to Move Slowly

[For the Student]

Remember to check in all directions every time you move the vehicle. Then proceed slowly, no more than about 25 kilometers an hour at first, and keep it under 40 for the duration of Step Two.

You want to begin to gain a comfortable feeling with the vehicle as you move a little faster than before, on a street instead of the parking lot. You want to move steadily and stop smoothly. Do not jam on the brake. Push in the pedal. For a smooth stop, ease off the pedal slightly before the vehicle stops moving.

Be patient. Take it easy. Master controlling the vehicle before you try for speed.

On Calm Streets

[For the Instructor]

Continue using called stops but be sure no other traffic is nearby when you do. As the student begins to explore quiet streets, she will experience the first driving encounters, although not frequently. Probable encounters will include:

- Occupied parking lots
- Stop signs
- Oncoming vehicles

Things to watch: improved parking skills, displaying more comfort with the steering wheel and the pedals, moving the vehicle in a straight line along the road, stopping precisely and executing simple interactions with other vehicles.

'Live' Parking Drills

Find a parking lot that is occupied and have the student practice pulling into spaces between two other vehicles. Exercise caution the first few times – and use the called stop if necessary – until she can enter a space without worry about bumping or even touching an adjoining vehicle.

Next, have her back out in each direction. And when you think the time is right, have the student try backing into a space, using the same technique you employed in the empty lot. This should be done slowly, of course, with the student looking through the rear window and guiding the back end of the vehicle into the space. Continue the drills until the student moves easily into and out of the parking spaces.

More Parking Practice

[For the Student]

When you pull into parking spaces where the adjoining spaces are occupied, your vehicle should be far enough out from the space that you can turn into it easily. If you have enough room, you should be able to pull straight in, leaving more or less equal space on both sides.

An Introduction to Safe Driving

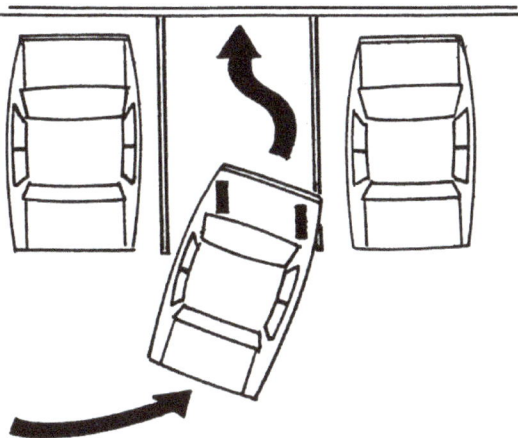

Most of the time, however, you will have to steer carefully into the space. The front corner of your vehicle should stay close to the adjoining vehicle on the outside of the turn. Follow along the side of that vehicle until you are about two-thirds of the way in. Then turn toward the center of the space and straighten out the wheels before you stop.

Do this slowly and carefully so there is no danger of scraping or bumping the other vehicle. When in doubt, stop, back out (after you **CLEAR THE WAY** behind you) and try again.

Stop Signs

Do not simply pull up to a stop sign. Its placement is an inexact process. If there is a crosswalk, stop in front of it. If not, pull up to the end of the street or road until you can see in all directions.

Keep your eyes ahead until you stop. If the view at the corner is blocked, watch out for pedestrians or cyclists moving into the crosswalk, particularly from the right.

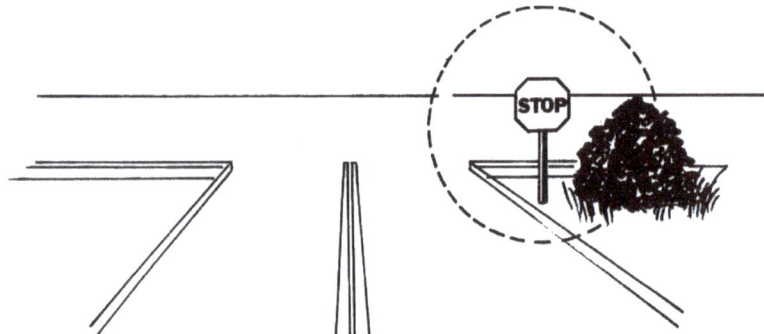

Many drivers, when they make right turns, tend to pull well into an intersection while looking left. If the view happens to be blocked on the right side, and they look left while turning right, they could miss someone and run right over them.

Signal if your intention is to turn then stop completely. Stop means stop. Look in all directions then pull out. Always remember: **CLEAR THE WAY**

First Encounters

If you are using side streets and back roads, they are likely to be narrow, so oncoming traffic can seem intimidating at first. The tendency of a beginning driver is to look at an oncoming vehicle. Do not. It tends to make you steer toward it.

For close encounters, keep your eyes mostly on the lane ahead.

Concentrate on the empty space but also pay some attention to the near front corner of the oncoming vehicle. It will provide an edge and the earliest warning that you do not have enough room to pass you by.

When in doubt, slow down or stop and let the other driver roll by you. At this stage, it will not hurt to interrupt things if necessary.

Turnarounds

[For the Instructor]

Find a dead-end two-lane street to begin practicing turnarounds. It is not a major maneuver, but it will help the student handle the vehicle more precisely in tight spaces.

The student should be able to reverse the vehicle's direction without backing up more than once and without bumping any curbs. Practice turnarounds several times until the student can execute them reliably.

Note: Do not try this anywhere but on a dead-end street.

Turning Around in Tight Spaces

[For the Student]

These are easy maneuvers because they are performed at low speed. Just remember three things:
1. Do not turn the steering wheel unless the vehicle is moving.
2. Always end each maneuver with the front wheels turned in the next direction you want to go.
3. Move slowly.

Start the turn as far to the right side of the roadway as possible. Turn sharply left, moving to the edge of the road. Straighten the wheel then turn right just before you stop. Keep the front wheels from hitting the curb. Back up with the wheels turned hard right then straighten out and turn left before you stop. Keep the rear wheels from hitting the curb.

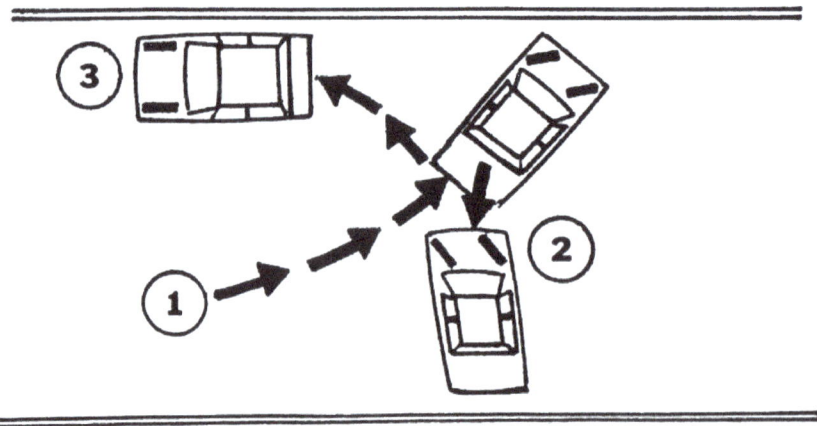

If you have completed the turnaround correctly, you should be able to pull away cleanly on your third move.

A Little Faster, A Little Busier

[For the Instructor]

Next, find an area that mixes neighborhood streets and minor traffic routes – but no four-lane highways. No road should have a speed limit higher than 55 kilometers per hour, and during Step Two the actual vehicle speed should be kept to 50 or under.

An ideal situation is a string of different neighborhoods that can be reached by crossing over, or driving briefly along, secondary two-lane routes. If there is a traffic light or two in the area, that would be fine, but you do not want too much traffic yet. The chief new ingredient here is more frequent encounters with other vehicles and with pedestrians.

The best arrangement would be to map out a circular route that can be repeated. Not too far; perhaps 15 kilometers or under.

You should not need to use the called stop as frequently – perhaps only once in a while, if necessary, to keep it available as an option. Once or twice, though, you might need to use it in earnest.

As the two of you drive through these areas, begin to discuss the possible hazards that can arise:
- Pedestrians. Is there plenty of room to allow them to cross safely ahead? Or, if they are walking along the road, is there enough room to go around them?
- Children playing in a yard. Are they playing with a ball that could roll into the street? Are they chasing one another so one of them could run in front of the vehicle?
- Hedges and walls. Could they conceal vehicles about to pull out of driveways?
- Occupants of parked vehicles on the side of the road. Are they about to open a door? Is there enough room to avoid them if they do?
- Approaching the top of a hill. Is there a vehicle stopped on the other side? Is someone standing in the middle of the road? Could the student stop the vehicle in time to avoid a hazard?
- Likewise, going around a blind curve in the road. What could be around the corner?

Here is an exercise I have used, and it seems to help train the student to think about possible hazards automatically. As you proceed along your designated route, ask the student to call out, as continuously as possible, each and every potential hazard she recognizes. If she misses any, speak up gently and point them out for her. Then repeat the route and the exercise until the student can spot all of the items she previously missed.

Learning to React

[For the student]

Whenever you encounter a situation that might be hazardous, you should react in the same way: Proceed with caution. How?

As soon as you notice something potentially hazardous, take your foot off the gas pedal. Lower your speed. This is important. You should do this anytime there is a possible obstruction or danger ahead. Almost every good driving maneuver begins with this action.

Keep your eyes on the object or area of concern. If it gets closer – and if there is no easy way to steer clear – then move your foot to the brake and press gently. Begin to slow down.

If there is no other choice, stop the vehicle.

For example, if you are approaching the top of a hill and your view of the road is shortened, you should slow down. Keep looking over the top. If something does appear suddenly, you will have time to deal with it. If the road is clear, you can steer around. If it is not, you can stop. Either way, by looking and slowing down you will have preserved your options.

If children in a yard begin moving toward the road in front of you, ease off the gas pedal in case you have to stop. Be aware of them until you pass by. If there is the slightest chance they will move in your path, stop. Never risk tragedy.

If an animal such as a red fox gets in a position to dash under the vehicle, ease off the gas. Animals can be unpredictable. Watch them.

Here is a tip about encountering animals near the road: Most animals cannot deal with vehicles. Their natural defenses are not prepared for a massive body that moves rapidly in a straight line. It baffles them. That is why so many end up underneath the wheels.
When you approach an animal near the road, ease off the gas. If the animal fails to move out of your way, slow down and tap your horn a couple of times, but not too loudly. You might scare it into shock. A couple of quick beeps usually will send most animals scampering away from the noise.

Dealing with Impatience

[For the Instructor]

It is unlikely that another vehicle will tailgate you in this environment. But on the road, anything is possible. If someone does display impatience or rudeness, find the earliest place to pull over and have the student signal and do so.

During Step Two, you want the student to slow down at the first sight of a possible hazard. You want to help her develop some sensitivity. A good way to do this is through exaggeration – by slowing down for everything. Later, when the student is more experienced, she will detect things more quickly and automatically and will know when to act. But for now, she should slow down for anything remotely hazardous. Therefore, you do not want anybody following you closely.

STEP THREE: Busy But Slow Encounters

[For the Instructor]

A good location to introduce your student to busy vehicular and pedestrian traffic is a shopping center parking lot. The reason is although such places are busy, the traffic speeds are low.

Find a parking lot that is suitable and, if necessary, drive the student there. Spend at least several sessions cruising the lanes and continuing to practice pulling into and out of parking spaces.

You will not be pursuing any new driving skills here. The purpose of Step Three is to get the student into the habit of noticing everything that is going on in the immediate area – to become sensitive to hazards in crowded places. It is something that will become more valuable later, when the real traffic encounters begin.

As you move around the lot, repeat the exercise you conducted during the circuitous route in the previous step: Ask the student to point out anything hazardous. Once again, do it in real time, so the student can get into the habit of spotting potential problems quickly, and prompt her if she misses something.

Add one new aspect: Anytime something causes her concern, suggest a way to deal with it. Repeat these sessions until she can pick things out nearly as quickly as you can. When she can complete an entire session without overlooking something – and react properly to everything, it will be time to move on.

One caution: Just because the speeds are low, do not assume this is a safe environment. Shopping center parking lots constitute a major source of fender-benders, because there is so much simultaneous activity, and because the rules are not as clearly defined as on the road. Teach the student to watch pedestrians and other drivers closely.

Low-Speed Hazards

[For the Student]

Even though you are driving slowly in a parking lot, plenty can go wrong:

- A car can pull out suddenly in front of you, either from a space or a crossing lane.
- A child or adult can dart out from between two cars into your path.
- If you are backing out of a parking space, you could back into a person or another vehicle.
- A vehicle or person could appear suddenly from around a corner.

Sharpen your skills by keeping an eye on everything around you as you drive. The key to doing it safely is to keep your speed low and be ready to react to anything that might happen.

Do Not Assume Anything

If, for example, you are about to drive past someone who is stopped and waiting to pull out, but that person is not looking at you, do not assume he or she will look before moving. Your best reaction: Take your foot off the gas.

Keep your eyes on the other party until you are seen. Otherwise, steer as wide a path as possible around the vehicle.

If you are approaching a vehicle that is ready to back out of a space (How can you tell? If the back-up lights are on, then the vehicle's gear shift is in "reverse.") do not assume the driver will wait for you to pass. Again, your best reaction is to take your foot off the gas. Watch the other vehicle's front wheel. If you see any movement, stop.

Your horn is a last resort. Never use it unless you must warn someone that they are about to bump you. Do not use it as a way to express disapproval. It is rude, and it makes people angry. Reserve it as a warning device only and tap it – do not hold on it.

Outside Then Inside

[For the Instructor]

Before you take the student to the streets, try one more variation on the busy parking lot: a busy parking garage. A parking garage offers new challenges, because the lanes tend to be narrower, and the spaces tend to be smaller. The entrance and exit ramps also are narrow, and garages require driving with the low-beam headlights on.

Remember: Low-speed places are not necessarily safe places. Careless and unskilled drivers are everywhere.

Have the student practice the same techniques in the garage that she had to employ in the outdoor lot. Continue to move along the lanes and pull into and out of, and back into, spaces. Always proceed slowly and carefully. Be sure when she backs out of a space that she backs out far enough to be able to make her next move easily and quickly.
Because this is a new environment, resume the hazard-spotting. When the student can maneuver through the garage well and call out all potential problems, you can move on.

But first...

A parking garage is a good place to begin talking about personal safety. Sometime soon, the student will obtain her license and might begin driving alone. That includes, sooner or later, entering a parking garage. You need to talk about choosing a parking space sensibly, such as avoiding isolation and dark corners and scanning the garage for suspicious characters. For example, tell her to be particularly aware – and to avoid – vans or vehicles with darkened windows.

Parking Garage Alert

[For the Student]

Never park next to a van or vehicle with darkened windows. If one is parked next to you, avoid entering your vehicle on that side. Enter on the opposite side or, better still as a precaution, wait until there are other people around before approaching your vehicle. This might seem too cautious, but it is a real danger related to many assaults on women in the United States.

As a general rule, always try to park in plain view of a busy entrance or pedestrian walkway. Your best situation in a parking garage is with people and in the light; the worst is isolation and darkness.

STEP FOUR: Stop and Go

[For the Instructor]

As soon as the student becomes accustomed to dealing with the slow traffic and commotion of busy parking lots and garages, you can move on to low-speed traffic in commercial strip areas, where there are frequent stop lights and lots of vehicles entering and exiting the road.

Low speed is the key factor here. Increase the interaction but maintain a moderate speed so the student can stop quickly if something goes wrong. Use roads and streets with speed limits of 55 kilometers an hour or under. Also, given the increased level of complexity, attempt Step Four only in daytime and good weather.

The traffic will be an important challenge, and the student should experience several new situations:
- Moving onto, off of and along commercial strip routes
- Stopping and starting at traffic lights
- Making right and left turns
- Maneuvering through roundabouts
- Changing lanes
- Learning to spot visual obstructions ("the canyon")

There is much to accomplish here, so take more time to complete Step Four than any of the first three steps. I recommend a minimum of five sessions before moving on.

Begin by mapping out a course that involves turning onto and off of a four-lane commercial route. Follow it for a few kilometers. Be sure the student stays in the right lane and drives at or near the (low) speed limit. Find a suitable (right) turnoff, such as a side street. Turn onto it, find a turnaround then reverse your course.

Whenever approaching a turnoff, make sure the student signals in plenty of time, slows down gradually and turns smoothly out of the traffic. Repeat this for perhaps a couple of hours. It is a way of providing a good introduction to driving in traffic.

This exercise should include the following situations:
- Turning smoothly into lanes and maintaining a steady position within a lane
- Maintaining a steady speed within traffic
- Maintaining proper distance behind vehicles and giving plenty of warning when turning or stopping
- Using the rearview and side mirrors to keep track of following and adjacent traffic
- Reacting quickly and properly when traffic lights turn yellow (coming to a stop unless the vehicle can cross the intersection easily before the light turns red)
- Paying attention so she does not hold up traffic when the light turns green
- Coming to a full stop, watching for cross traffic and turning right on red
- Watching out for red-light runners
- Avoiding pulling abruptly ahead when the side view is blocked by larger vehicles such as trucks and vans

Make sure the student experiences everything on the list and handles each one well. All the while, continue to practice hazard-spotting, just like you did in Step Three. Same rules: Continue until the student spots everything and handles every situation properly.

Dealing with Traffic

[For the Student]

The task here is to combine two skills: scanning for hazards and reacting to them and blending in with traffic in a steady and predictable way. You can do this by extending your attention as far ahead and behind as possible and comfortable.

CLEAR THE WAY

How? If you spend too much time and effort trying to identify hazards, will it make you nervous? Will it become tiring?

Not if you do it properly.

First, look well ahead of your vehicle. Do not focus on the pavement or on the vehicle in front of you. Instead, try to maintain a relaxed, general gaze forward. Do not stare. Let your eyes move around naturally. Glance at the mirrors frequently but keep your main attention in front of you.

Second, do not press. Try to relax. You are developing the ability to use your peripheral vision as your early warning system. Use it to create an imaginary CLEAR ZONE that extends in all directions from your vehicle. You will not be able to do this right away. It will take time before it operates automatically, but if you practice it every time you drive it will become a habit.

Making a CLEAR ZONE

Peripheral vision is the most effective tool you have to protect yourself. It is also the least-tiring way because it uses the natural abilities of your body. We humans have the capacity to recognize inconsistencies in our environment, inconsistencies that instantly attract our attention.

Inconsistencies? Yes, such as something that moves. Or, something that is different from its surroundings – something that contrasts or reflects, either lighter or darker.

You can make good use of this ability while driving. When you are moving along in your vehicle, whether in traffic or alone, the road and the landscape take on a consistent and predictable pattern. The pavement passes beneath your vehicle in a certain way. The sidewalks, street lamps and road signs pass by in this way as well. If you drive properly, you blend into the flow of traffic. Everyone moves along at basically the same speed. It becomes a moving CLEAR ZONE.

Within the zone, everything is fine. You are relaxed. It is only when something changes that you snap to a higher level of attention:
- Someone changes lanes in front of you.
- Someone signals to turn
- Someone applies the brakes.
- Someone pulls out in front of you from the right.
- Someone pulls out from the left into the lane beside you.
- A bird darts across the road at low altitude.

Any actions like these require an immediate reaction from you, so you must notice what is happening immediately. Then, most times, you need only ease off the gas. The same with anything that happens along the side of the road or on the pavement itself:

- A pedestrian waits to cross the street.
- A vehicle waits to pull out of a parking lot or side street.
- A bicyclist rides along the right side of the lane.
- A pothole appears in the lane ahead.

Such things represent inconsistencies with the normal pattern of traffic, pavement or scenery. In a sense, they have invaded your CLEAR ZONE. As soon as they appear, they should attract your attention. Whether you approach them, or they approach you, keep your attention focused on them so you can react as quickly as possible if necessary.

The most important thing is to notice potential hazards quickly. The sooner you recognize them, the more time you will have available to react. Why is this so important? Because it takes time and distance to bring a vehicle to a stop. If you do not have enough time or distance, and you have no room to steer out of the way, then you are going to hit something. This is simple but important. Lack of time to react is the first component of a crash.

Consider this: If you are traveling at 55 kilometers an hour, you will need approximately 50 meters to stop. That is one-half the length of a soccer field. At 55, you are traveling over 15 meters per second.

Yes, every second elapsed means at least 15 meters traveled. By the time you notice something, recognize what it is, move your foot to the brake, apply pressure to the brake, and brake the vehicle to a stop, about three seconds will have passed. Three seconds is as fast as anyone can stop in that situation, and three seconds at 55 kilometers an hour means nearly 50 meters. The faster you go, the more stopping distance required. That is why you must keep your attention well ahead.

By the way, if someone pulls or merges into an adjoining lane, what is the quickest way to tell if that vehicle is moving into your lane? By watching its front wheel. If it is turned properly, it is not headed into your CLEAR ZONE, so the vehicle is no hazard.

Do Not Violate Your Own CLEAR ZONE
Remember, it is always possible to get into trouble by failing to spot an obstruction. Typical trouble can happen at a stop sign or stop light in a line of vehicles waiting to make right turns.

The problem occurs when someone ahead of you is waiting to turn. If you look left at oncoming traffic and forget to check whether the vehicle in front of you has actually pulled away – BAM! Many fender-benders have resulted from this situation. So, if you are looking left and the road is clear, do not forget about what is directly in front of you. CLEAR THE WAY.

Along the Strip

[For the Instructor]

Make at least several passes back and forth along your designated course during each lesson. Try to do it when there is moderate but not heavy traffic. The student should stay in the right lane. Attempt no major interactions yet. Merely allow her to become accustomed to the sensory input of rolling along a somewhat busy thoroughfare.
Watch out, however, for drivers pulling out suddenly from side streets and parking lots, and for drivers who take too much time turning off the roadway. Train the student to anticipate these mistakes in other drivers.

Continue to be the co-pilot and keep up the hazard-spotting as long as necessary. Also, watch the line the student maintains. That is, she should be following the contours of the road in a smooth way. No weaving within the lane.

The same with speed: steady and consistent with gradual starts and stops. No acting like a race driver, and no screeching to a halt.

Stop Light? Drive Light

[For the Student]

When a traffic light turns red ahead, ease off the gas and coast to the stop as much as possible. No need to burn excess gasoline to go nowhere. Many drivers – young and old – tend to hold their speed until the last possible moment when they approach a stop sign or light. Some people actually try to pass other vehicles before getting there. This is wasteful and sometimes dangerous.

If the traffic light has already turned red, ease up. Hurry-up-and-wait is a useless activity. Remember to ease off the brake pedal just as your vehicle stops.

Watch Out for Red-Light Runners
One common hazard at controlled intersections is drivers who try to rush through them before the light turns red, only to fail. Or, sometimes drivers will even ignore red lights. It is a pervasive problem – though the Saher system seems to be having a positive effect. Nevertheless, you should not start out the instant your light turns green. You could move into the intersection and be broadsided by a red-light runner.

When you are stopped at an intersection and the light turns green, always CLEAR THE WAY. Check both directions before moving.

Increase the Complexity

[For the Instructor]

When the student reaches good confidence and skill levels with this exercise, begin to incorporate more complicated maneuvers:

- Turning right into a parking lot, finding a space and pulling in then backing out and returning to the strip, turning right onto it.
- Changing lanes and making a left turn, first at a traffic light with a left-turn arrow, next at a light without a left arrow, and last at an entrance to something without a light. Left turns should be practiced at first behind, then in front of, oncoming traffic – if there is enough time and distance to do so.
- Returning to the strip and making a left turn onto it.

These exercises will require more skill and judgment, so be cautious. If the student is having trouble adjusting to the new challenges, ease off a little. Return to the maneuvers she was performing well and attempt to rebuild her confidence before returning to more complex items.

This process is about adapting gradually to new situations and building good habits. Every beginning driver will progress at her own rate. There is always a little nervousness at each new situation, but you should judge whether the student is proceeding through the exercises too quickly.

If there is any doubt, allow extra time. Too much time spent at any of these stages is better than too little. Make sure the student performs each new skill well before moving on.

Roundabouts

[For the Student]

Many of the world's cities use a configuration intended to merge vehicle traffic that is arriving from several or even many directions simultaneously. It is called a roundabout, and though it might seem intimidating at first it is relatively easy to master. Designed like an old-fashioned wagon wheel, the converging streets are the spokes and the central traffic circle is the hub. Your task is to enter and exit the hub smoothly.

A roundabout's advantage is that all traffic within its hub moves in the same direction – in your country's case, counterclockwise. This eliminates the need to track traffic from two or more directions at once. When approaching a roundabout, here is what to do:

- Ignore the traffic within the hub at first. Make sure no vehicles are stopped ahead of you and waiting to merge.
- If the way is blocked, wait patiently for your turn but also keep checking your rearview mirror to see if the drivers behind have seen that you are stopped.
- As soon as the way forward is open, watch for a space in the hub's outer lane (the lane nearest you) and move into it.

- If you will be exiting soon, stay in the outer lane and exit promptly.
- For this exercise, even if you need to pass by many "spokes" of the wheel, stay in the outer lane. You want to maintain simplicity for now.

Changing Lanes

These maneuvers are relatively easy in terms of the physical skill required. They can be completed with only a slight turn of the wheel. Lane changes should not be abrupt, but they also should not take too long, either – just smooth slides over to the left or right.

Make sure no one is about to stop suddenly in front of you. Put your signal on and check the mirrors. Even if everything seems clear...

Do not shift lanes just yet.
Many crashes occur in just such situations. The reason is the blind spots in your mirrors, particularly if they are not positioned properly. People glance at the mirrors, assume it is safe to change lanes, and suddenly feel the impact of a collision. So, hold your lane for just a moment, turn your head and quickly look at the adjoining lane.

CLEAR THE WAY

If it is clear, move over smoothly then turn your signal off. Do it every time you change lanes. The same with moving to the right:

- Turn your signal on.
- Check the mirrors.
- Glance to the right.

All clear? Change lanes. Signal off.

Many modern vehicles now feature lane-change sensors that will alert you if there is another vehicle in your path. Some vehicles even have control systems that will prevent you from changing lanes if a collision is imminent. But no automatic system operates perfectly. Whether or not your vehicle offers these advantages, learn to rely on your own eyes and reflexes.

Left Turns

When you attempt left turns at controlled intersections – first with left turn lanes and arrows and then without such guidance – move into the proper lane well before it is time to turn.

An Introduction to Safe Driving

As you approach the intersection, put your turn signal on at least five seconds before you reach the place to turn. Do this even if you are moving in a "Left Turn Only" lane. You need to be perfectly predictable.

Sometimes streets are designed to permit two lanes at a time to turn left. If so, it is important to maintain your lane all the way through the turn – you do not want to drift into someone.

This is another situation where looking ahead will serve you well. As you turn, focus on where you want to go. Stay in the center of the lane.

Making Turns with Caution

[For the Instructor]

Turning left in front of oncoming traffic can be tricky. In fact, it can be dangerous. The student needs to be able to judge speed and distance with accuracy. The first few times, provide close guidance. She must develop a sense of when to move.

At this early stage of building skills, keep oncoming traffic 10 seconds away before giving the student the all-clear. Do not cut it close. Allow plenty of time. If there is any doubt, wait. Later on, you can cut the lead time down to about three seconds.

Also important when turning: Have the student keep the wheels straight until beginning the turn. If you are sitting with your wheels turned to the left, and someone hits you from behind, they could push you into oncoming traffic.

Look for the Empty Space

[For the Student]
When you need to turn left behind oncoming traffic, focus your attention on the space behind that traffic. Do not look directly at an oncoming vehicle. Drive into the empty space behind it.

A good guideline for making left turns in front of traffic is what I call the 3-Second Rule. That is, after you complete your turn – meaning you are completely out of the way of oncoming traffic – if it takes at least 3 seconds for that traffic to cross in your rearview mirror, then you have turned in plenty of time.

Avoid 'The Canyon'
There is a hazard that can develop that has nothing to do with the roadside or the pavement. I call it "the canyon." It happens anytime your sideways vision is blocked because there is a larger vehicle such as a truck or a bus beside you, or maybe even on both sides.

This can be hazardous even when you are stopped or when you are approaching a cross street. You have to be careful not to jump out in front suddenly, because there might be a vehicle – such as a red-light runner – or a pedestrian about to cross in front of you. The driver in the truck or bigger vehicle can see. You cannot.

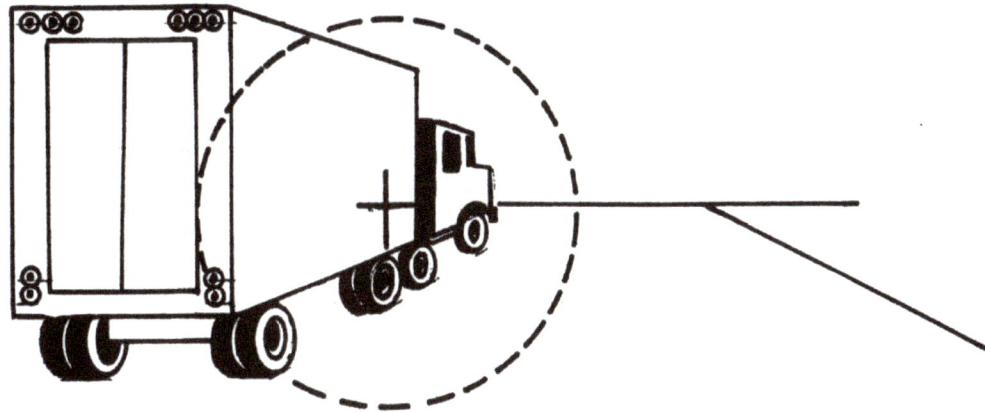

Do one of two things here:

1. Wait until the big vehicle starts moving. Roll alongside it until you are through the intersection then move ahead.
2. If you are trying to make a right turn, and the left lane is obstructed, move out slowly until you can see that no traffic or pedestrian is approaching from the left.

Avoiding the canyon is just one more variation of CLEAR THE WAY.

Do Not Follow Large Vehicles Too Closely
The Canyon can also appear behind larger vehicles if you fail to keep a proper distance behind them. Stay back far enough until you can see what is going on farther down the street or road.

Teach Navigation

[For the Instructor]

It might seem obvious, but do not assume the student knows how to find destinations along streets and roads or can determine the best route to get somewhere.

When I was teaching one of my daughters, I told her one day to drive to a shopping center located about three miles from our house. It was a destination completely familiar to her. But she shocked me when she asked how to get there.

"Why?" I asked. "We have been going there for years."

"Yes," she replied, "but you always drove, so I never paid attention to how we got there."

It would not hurt, in this and future steps, to have the student practice following directions and finding street addresses as part of the lessons. GPS and the other onboard navigation systems have made finding things easier. Nevertheless, knowing how to read a map and determine directions the old-fashioned way is still a valuable skill.

Also, spend some time explaining your hometown's system of street numbers and street names. This likewise can be a big help to a beginner as she drives to destinations for the first time.

A Special Note About Center Turn Lanes

[For the Student]

Occasionally, you will encounter a road with a center turn lane. The center lane is used for left turns, but it is potentially hazardous because oncoming traffic can converge there. The danger results whenever you are in the center lane, moving toward a left turn that is beyond an oncoming vehicle also moving in the lane. If neither of you pays attention, you could have a head-on collision.

If you are on a road with a center turn lane, and you need to make a left turn, do not cruise the center lane. Wait until you are almost at the turn. Signal, check your blind spot and the lane ahead for traffic then move over, continuing to watch for oncoming vehicles. You want to minimize your time in the center lane.

STEP FIVE: Countryside

[For the Instructor]

[Note: *I created this section for my book about teaching American teenagers to drive because even in the most densely populated metropolitan areas in the United States there is still plenty of adjoining rural countryside. Depending on your particular location in the Kingdom, you might want to skip this step if finding such destinations is not convenient – although I would recommend that the student receive some training in rural or mountainous areas sometime early in her driving experience*.]

In the previous step, you introduced the student to the bustling and frequently nerve-wracking environment of traffic. Most of the challenge involved interacting with and avoiding other vehicles at relatively low speeds.

Next, you should spend some time working with the student on developing pure driving skills, on getting used to various types of roads and terrain, on feeling more comfortable in the vehicle, and on experiencing all of the physical motions that driving requires. It should be a more pleasant experience than the shopping strip district: less traffic, more scenery. But do not let your guard down. Plenty of hazards reside in the countryside.

You will want to find an area that is sparsely populated and not well-traveled. Find some lengthy two-lane roads that wind through the landscape but are not main arteries. Roads with many curves and hills are desirable. The top speed for this section is about 75 kilometers an hour.

You will need to continue the co-piloting and hazard-spotting, except that most of it should involve the road and the landscape. I would advise not to try passing unless it is absolutely necessary, and you should confine the lessons to good weather and daylight.

As long as there are no major highways or arteries, the student can drive to the area you have selected. You will be teaching about highways later, but she is still inexperienced and does not belong in traffic at highway speeds.

In Step Five, we will work on these specific skills:
- Following the contour of the road
- Strengthening peripheral vision
- Adjusting speed as necessary for curves and hills, alternating between the gas and the brake
- Identifying new potential hazards
- Reading and understanding road signs

Driving Is Sensing

[For the Student]

The process of driving is about three-fourths sensory and one-fourth logical. It greatly resembles a sport: Most of it is automatic, and the higher brain functions do not govern. When you have mastered driving, you will not actively think your way along the road:

"I want to turn right, so I should move the wheel in that direction. Yes, that is far enough. Now I need to straighten out."

Instead, your eyes recognize the path your brain wants to follow. Without thinking consciously and deliberately, your brain orders your hands to turn the wheel along that path. It orders your feet to press on the gas or the brake so that the speed of the vehicle is proper for the condition of the road.

Thinking comes in when you reach a fork in the road and decide which one to take. Or, when you begin to feel tired and decide it is time to stop for a break. Or, most frequently, when a hazard presents itself in the distance and you have time to decide how to deal with it.

When something happens quickly, however, you must react reflexively. The habits and skills must be well-developed to protect you, but they will not become well-developed unless you practice every maneuver.

So, do not assume that because you are now moving onto roadways you are ready for anything. You are not. Be patient. You have a long way to go.

Take the Time

[For the Instructor]

If you decide to apply this section to the driving lessons, plan on spending perhaps as many as 10 sessions driving through the countryside, an hour or so each time. This will help the student's mind and body become more accustomed to this process. Basically, it is a hand-eye coordination drill.

Looking Well Ahead

[For the Student]

In order to follow the contour of the road as smoothly as possible, you need to keep your eyes well ahead of the vehicle. If you look ahead, you will tend to steer a very smooth course in the center of the lane. If you shorten your focus, you will begin to weave.

You are driving at a higher speed now, so your stopping distance will be increased. At about 75 kilometers an hour, you will need at least 60 meters to stop, so you should be looking at least that far ahead.

When you are driving through the countryside, however, there will be times when you are unable to see that far: around a blind curve, for example, or over the top of a hill. Therefore, if you cannot see 60 meters ahead, and if it would take you at least 60 meters to stop, then your CLEAR ZONE has disappeared. You are in an unsafe situation.

What do you do?

Anytime your visibility decreases, slow down. If you can see only 50 meters ahead, you should be doing no more than 55. If visibility drops to 30 meters, your speed should slow to 40, and so on. Remember: You need to recognize a hazard and move your foot to the brake in time to make a safe stop. Always reduce speed until your CLEAR ZONE matches or exceeds your speed.

Check Your Speed

By the way, how do you know how fast you are going? Check your speedometer once in a while – but only for an instant. If you look away from the road, you are driving blind for the duration of that look. At 75 kilometers an hour, a one-second look translates into 20 meters of blind travel. Keep your glances short and only when the road ahead is clear.

Handling Curves Correctly

[For the Instructor]

Try to emphasize three things every time the student encounters a curve:

- Entering a curve at the proper speed, so there is no need to brake harshly to prevent skids or loss of control
- Developing a keen sense of the arc of the curve, so the vehicle remains in the center of the lane all the way through
- Watching the inside edge of the curve (looking around the curve), which is the quickest way to detect sudden hazards

If the student is performing correctly, the vehicle will track smoothly in the center of the lane. If the student's focus is too short, the vehicle will weave through the turn, requiring steering corrections.

Looking and Curving

[For the Student]

As I keep mentioning, it is always best to look ahead while you are driving, but not too far. Gaze too far ahead and you could miss important details that are closer to you. Try to maintain your attention about 5 seconds down the road. For now, 5 seconds is plenty of time to recognize a hazard and react to it.

How do you tell what is 5 seconds ahead? Pick an object that you pass alongside the road. Count slowly to five and look in your rearview mirror to see how far away it has become.

Now, pick out something ahead that seems the same distance away. Count to five again. If you practice, soon you will figure it out. And if you keep practicing, after a while, you will know instinctively the best distance to look ahead at any speed.

Do not stare at the same place on the road. Your eyes work best when they do not fix on something for long periods. You have to keep looking mostly far ahead while glancing frequently at other things.

Curves are different, because often they restrict your view. If you encounter curves, keep your attention on each curve's inside edge as far ahead as possible, and you will steer the course correctly. When you see the curve ending, resume normal speed and normal looking ahead.

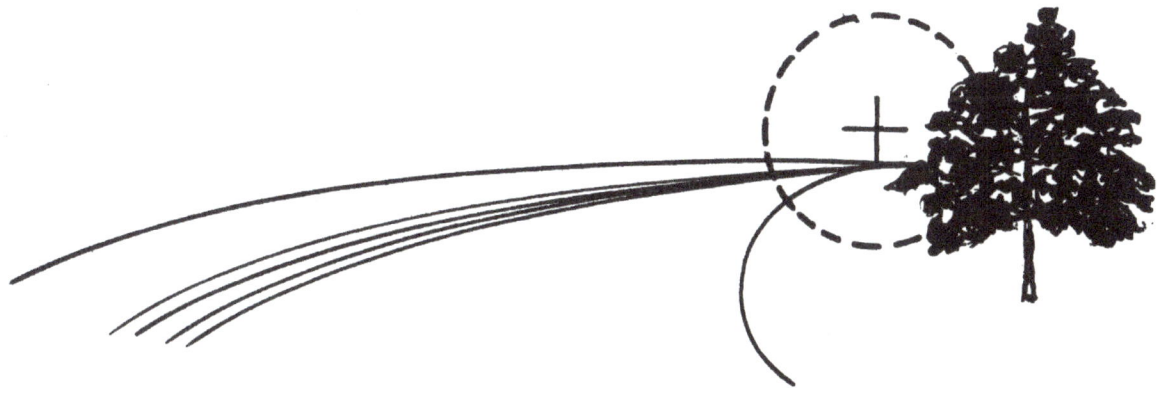

Remember the following about curves:
- Slow down before you enter the curve.
- Look around the bend, concentrating on the inside edge.

- Do not restrict your review to the windshield. If the road curves sharply, look out the side window as well to keep watching the curve's inside edge.
- Stay in your lane all the way through the curve (on a curve to the left, do not cheat into the oncoming lane).
- Resume speed as you re-enter the straightaway.

Watch for Loss of Control

[For the Instructor]

Take extra care with the student on curves and hilltops. Not only is visibility restricted, but inertia also will begin to affect the vehicle. This can be frightening to someone who has not experienced it before; it can lead to sudden loss of control. I remember the first time, as a young and beginning driver, I felt my vehicle slide around a curve on a dirt road. I did not realize that I had been going too fast to take the curve safely. As a result, because of my inexperience I overreacted and plowed into an embankment. The damage was minor, but the fear I felt was intense.

Maintaining control involves learning how much speed is prudent on a particular curve on a particular type of road. The correct speed depends on visibility, pavement conditions and stability of the vehicle. Beginning drivers do not know this yet, and it is difficult to teach, because it involves an acute sense of the limits of the vehicle in a given set of circumstances. That sense must be developed over time; it is the product of experience.

Until the student acquires that sense, it is usually best for you to make the judgments. When you think it is necessary, tell the student to slow down – before entering the curve. Train her to slow down whenever the situation feels uncomfortable.

Theme Two of Five: LEARN THE LIMITS

[For the Student]

Curves can be tricky, because physical forces act on the vehicle – forces called inertia and gravity.

An Introduction to Safe Driving

When you begin turning the wheel, the vehicle's momentum wants to keep it headed in a straight line. Gravity holds the vehicle to the ground, and the tires grip the road, but inertia causes the vehicle to lean away from the turn.

Inertia also pulls you and everyone in the vehicle to one side or another during the turn – you can feel it.

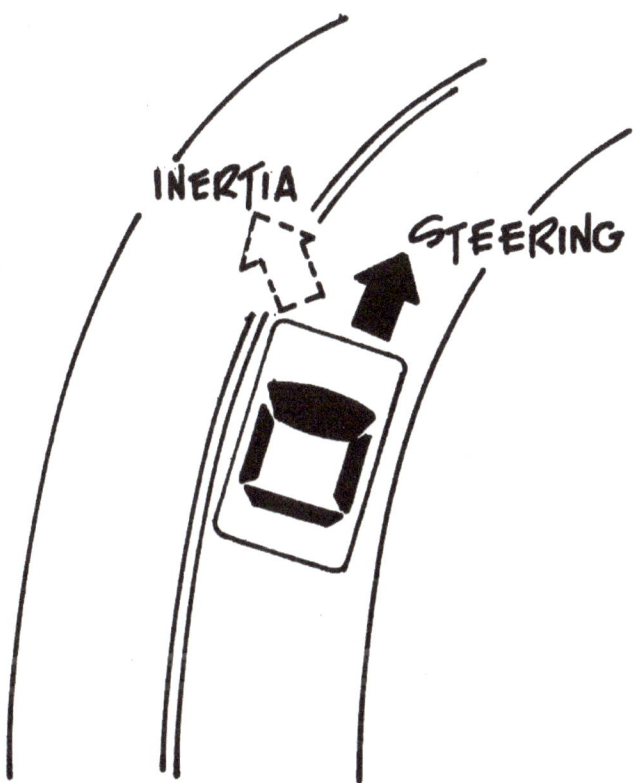

It sounds technical, but basically you need to know that the faster you try to go around a turn, the more powerful inertia becomes. Gravity and friction remain constant, so at some point inertia becomes too strong and you lose control on the turn – you skid, or even fly, off the road.

Banking – the sideways slope of the roadway – also affects inertia. A properly banked curve reduces the effects of inertia. An improperly banked road exacerbates it.

How can you know all this? Well, you cannot, not right away. It takes time to LEARN THE LIMITS, which is the second of our five themes. Until then, you can only keep safe by being cautious. Approach curves and turns at a comfortable speed. As you gain experience, you will learn more about what a vehicle can and cannot do under certain conditions.

In order to complete a turn safely, inertia either must be reduced or overcome. Most of the overcoming is accomplished by the friction between the road surface and the tire treads. Part of it also involves the strength of the vehicle's structure, which keeps it from falling apart, because the wheels are pulling one way and inertia is pulling another.

If the vehicle has a low center of gravity, it can take a tight turn at high speed without rolling over. Vehicles with higher centers of gravity, such as SUVs, have a greater chance of a rollover.

The type of pavement can affect this process as well. Asphalt or concrete will provide enough friction between the tires and the road, allowing the vehicle to hold the turn. Gravel, dirt or sand, however, offer a lower degree of friction, so the vehicle cannot hold a turn as well. Losing friction means losing control and sliding out of the lane.

Several other road conditions can cause tires to lose "traction," as it is called:
- Water, from rainfall or flooding
- Wet leaves
- Ice and snow
- Oil or other viscous fluids

If you encounter any of these unexpectedly on a curve, you will slide right off if you are not prepared. Road friction is no longer strong enough to overcome inertia.

I explained that inertia could be reduced as well as overcome. The best way to reduce inertia is to slow down, and the best time to slow down is before you enter the curve.

The same can be true at the tops of hills, although limited visibility is a much more frequent problem.

Still, it is important to remember the same forces that can cause you to lose control on curves also can operate on hilltops. On some rural roads, taking an abrupt hilltop too fast can cause the tires to lift off the surface of the road.

Whenever the tires lose contact there is no control at all. You are then at the mercy of whatever is waiting on the other end of your mistake.

When you LEARN THE LIMITS, you will know what the vehicle can and cannot do safely under certain conditions. You will know how fast you can take a turn when the pavement is solid, gravelly, dry or wet.

How can you LEARN THE LIMITS?
Practice, practice. And more practice.

Until then, you cannot know. The smartest thing to do is slow down before you become involved in a situation you cannot control, where things can get out of control very, very quickly.

Fortunately, modern vehicles are equipped with antilock braking systems (ABS), which can add to your margin of safety. ABS allows braking without locking the wheels – something that can immediately throw the vehicle into a skid. As long as the wheels are turning, the tire treads can transfer much of the energy from the vehicle's inertia – its momentum – to the road, and you can remain in control.

ABS permits you to correct your speed if you have entered a curve too fast. If this has happened, and you feel the vehicle being pulled forcefully to one side, push on the brake pedal to slow down but also continue to steer around the curve.

You can tell if you are taking a turn properly if you can maintain a steady speed through it and if you do not have to correct your steering. Keep looking well ahead through turns, concentrating on the inside of the curve, because it gives you the earliest sign of a hazard.

Countryside Hazards

[For the Instructor]

As you and the student cruise the countryside, you will need to point out all of the new potential hazards she will encounter:

- Oncoming traffic (Again, try not to expose her to too much of this, because it is a new situation where the other vehicles are traveling faster)
- Road squeezes (zones by guardrails or other obstructions)
- Tractors and farm or construction machinery on the road or crossing it
- Large wild animals or livestock

- Hidden driveways
- Cross-country cyclists
- Pedestrians
- Railroad crossings

Each of these will require a different response, so be ready to give guidance quickly.

Countryside Cruising

[For the Student]

You will be using your hands and feet frequently in these drills. Rolling across country roads requires frequent changes in speed and direction. It is the best way to sharpen your abilities to steer, brake and spot hazards. You will know you are doing well in these exercises if your changes in speed and your turns are smooth and gradual. If so, you are reacting properly to everything on the road.

I will cover more on this later, but for now, concentrate on two things:
1. Steering precisely and smoothly to follow the contour of the road.
2. Working your right foot back and forth easily from the gas pedal to the brake.

Regarding the gas and the brake, you have four movements to choose:
1. Ease off the gas (the most frequent move).
2. Move to the brake.
3. Ease on the brake.
4. Depress the brake fully.

On a smooth, straight highway, you might not need to use any of these movements for long periods, but on a curving, hilly country road, your foot will be moving almost constantly.

How do you decide what to do? As with steering, look where you want to go, and your hands will follow. Concentrate also on your CLEAR ZONE and your foot will follow. You want to be able to stop or steer clear if you need to, so you are going to have to adjust your vehicle's speed frequently to match the situation.

- Take your foot off the gas as a precaution – just in case.
- Move your foot to the brake when you are ready to stop.

Whether you use the other two moves (easing on the brake and depressing the brake fully) depends on what happens in front of you.

Can you think about all this? No. You must practice it until you develop a good sense of what to do. Then, you can do it all the time without thinking.

Practice, practice and more practice.

Oncoming Traffic

On a two-lane road, oncoming traffic will seem more intimidating to you because of the speeds you will be traveling. You have good reason to feel that way. At 55 kilometers an hour each, for example, two vehicles approach each other at a combined speed of 110. Even with the best seat belts and airbags, a head-on collision at that velocity can be extremely dangerous.

It is important to maintain a steady course within your lane. No need to move to the right as an oncoming vehicle approaches. Hold your position. As it passes, keep looking at the road beyond it but notice its near edge. Again, that edge provides the earliest indication it might be too close to you.

Beware of Road Squeezes

A potentially dangerous hazard lurks often in plain sight along rural roads. Here are some examples of how it can suddenly appear:

- The road crosses a creek or a dry wash, and traffic in both directions is protected by guardrails installed near the pavement, or the road passes over a narrow bridge.

- A curve on a hillside is flanked by a rock outcropping near the lane in one direction and a guardrail preventing a steep drop-off on the other.
- The road in both directions features wide shoulders, but disabled or parked vehicles block access to those shoulders for a short distance.

In all such cases, if you encounter these hazards, and if something causes oncoming traffic to move into your lane, you will suddenly lack an escape route – your only option might be to stop suddenly and suffer a head-on collision at the lowest possible speed.

I will discuss an emergency escape maneuver later. For now, the best practice in a situation like this is to learn to recognize road squeezes when they appear and do your best to avoid entering them at the same time as oncoming traffic – slow down as much as possible – and be ready to react at the instant a collision seems imminent.

Beware of Drop-Offs
Another dangerous situation that can develop almost instantly along a country road, particularly during your learning months, is called a drop-off. As with a road squeeze, if you respond to it the wrong way it can be deadly.

A drop-off occurs when your front wheel suddenly moves from the pavement onto a shoulder that is lower than the road. It could have happened because you took a curve too quickly. Or, you somehow allowed the vehicle to drift off the pavement. Whatever the cause, a drop-off is noisy and disturbing.

It can become dangerous if you obey your first instinct, which is to jerk the wheel sharply back toward the road. Do not! It can cause the vehicle to whip sideways and cross into the oncoming lane.

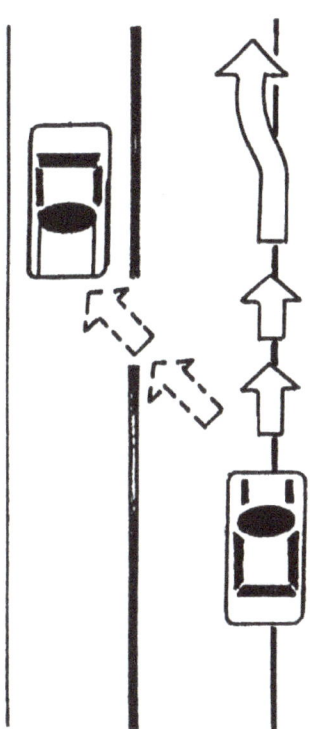

Instead, remember that piece of advice I have been repeating all along: At the first sign of trouble, ease off the gas. Do not hit the brakes. Then, move the vehicle a little farther to the right.

Yes, move right – but slightly. You want to get the right-front wheel away from the edge of the pavement, where it might veer suddenly to the left and force you across the road. Keep the front wheels parallel to the road until you slow down and then gradually steer the vehicle back onto the pavement.

This is important, so let me go over it again:
- At the first sign of a drop-off, ease off the gas.
- Avoid hitting the brakes.
- Move a little farther to the right, away from the edge of the pavement.
- Steer parallel to the road until you slow down.
- Gently ease back onto the pavement.

The critical thing is not to panic. It will make for a bumpy ride, but if you handle it correctly a drop-off will be temporary and a minor inconvenience.

Practicing a Drop-Off

[For the Instructor]

The danger of an overreaction to a drop-off is so great that it is a good idea to practice dealing with it a few times. Experience is the best teacher, but it should be attempted only on an empty road. Here is what you need:

- A stretch where the shoulder drops a few centimeters off the pavement
- Good visibility, so there is no chance of traffic, either following or oncoming, appearing unexpectedly
- Familiarity with the recovery procedure

At low speed, have the student move the vehicle off the road then recover. Do this several times, gradually increasing the speed until the student can perform it smoothly at about 55 kilometers an hour. But watch out for traffic!

Other Countryside Hazards

[For the Student]

If a farm tractor is crossing the road, the most important thing is to spot it in time. If you are maintaining a sufficient CLEAR ZONE in front of you, there should be no problem.

If the machine is moving ahead of you, chances are it is moving slowly. The CLEAR ZONE should detect it in time. Slow down gradually behind it. Wait until the road ahead is clear then accelerate smoothly and pass.

Cattle, camels, dromedaries, tahrs and other large animals near the road can be unpredictable. Do not assume they will not suddenly move in front of you. Slow down until you can stop in time if needed then ease past them. Use short taps on your horn to drive animals away.

Hidden driveways are a constant possibility in rural America; in the outlying areas of Saudi Arabia not so much, but where they exist the CLEAR ZONE should take care of them. If a driveway or entrance is hidden, it means overall visibility is reduced, which means your CLEAR ZONE is reduced. Slow down until it expands again.

Theme Three of Five: SHARE THE ROAD

Countryside cruising is a good place to learn the third of five themes: SHARE THE ROAD. It means you should use common courtesy wherever and whenever you can. Give others a break – cyclists, for example. Cyclists usually travel on the right edge of the lane but not the shoulder of the road. Whenever you see them, ease up as you pass them, and pass them only if there is plenty of room. Do not crowd. Many roads have rough shoulders or drop-offs that could spill a cyclist.

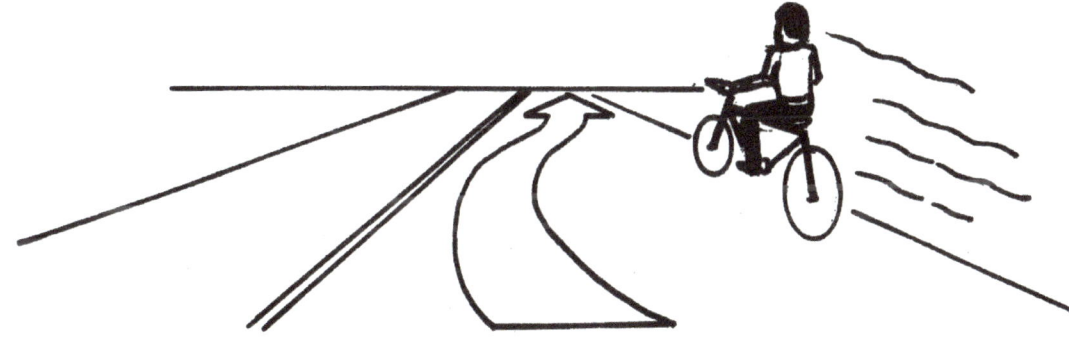

Move to the left to increase the margin of safety. If you cannot pass immediately, be patient. The same goes for pedestrians. Ease up until you pass them, move left to give them room, and do not pass unless it is safe – for the pedestrians and for you. SHARE THE ROAD is an essential part of good driving.

The Special Danger of Railroad Crossings
We have thousands of what are called at-grade railroad crossings in the United States, meaning vehicles literally must cross over railroad tracks. Some are guarded by flashing signals and automated gates, which lower when trains approach. Others are guarded by signals only. And some offer neither gates nor signals. You have fewer of these in your country, but all deserve your careful

attention. Motorists are killed every year because they do not take the crossings seriously. Or, they mistakenly assume that a train can stop before it hits them.

Never – never – cross a railroad track unless you can see that it is clear, in both directions.

What if you cannot see all the way down the tracks? Stop the vehicle, roll down your window and listen! If you hear a train approaching but cannot see it, do not move. If you cannot see it, you cannot tell how fast it is moving.

If there is more than one track, and a train has passed, do not move unless you can see all the way in both directions on both tracks. Again, if you cannot see, remain stopped and listen.

Make no mistake. People die regularly at railroad crossings. If you tangle with a train, you will lose. Even if the tracks are clear, always make sure the road ahead is clear on the other side. You never want to get stuck on the tracks. People have died that way, too.

Beware of Tailgaters

[For the Instructor]

Even though you and the student are driving along roads with light traffic, sometimes vehicles will pull up behind you and follow closely. Get the student in the habit of checking the rearview mirror regularly, at least several times each minute. If someone approaches closely from behind, take the first available turnoff.

Read the Road Signs

[For the Student]

When you drive through the countryside, road signs take on added importance. They help you by identifying conditions and possible hazards beyond your vision. Whenever you see a road sign, make sure you read it and understand it. A guide to your country's road signs can be found easily via a web search. Study them to make sure you recognize all of them.

Turning onto Roadways

[For the Instructor]

One other important countryside exercise is pulling out from a stop onto a road, both right and left. It requires caution and judgment, so have the student practice it frequently and carefully each time. It is not difficult to imagine what could go wrong in such a situation, particularly when visibility is limited. The key to safety is looking continuously.

Getting Up to Speed

[For the Student]

Whenever you have to pull out from a stop to the right, be sure to CLEAR THE WAY to the right. Make certain no one is about to walk or bike in front of you. Then look left and pull out if the lane is clear. Make sure you accelerate smoothly until you reach cruising speed. Many inexperienced drivers when pulling out tend to think they have completed the maneuver as soon as they complete the turn. So they poke along, taking too much time to get up to speed. Doing so lacks regard for overtaking traffic. Neglecting to get up to speed properly interferes with the flow of traffic. It is not a smart thing to do.

When you turn left, you have a more complex task because you have to be aware of traffic approaching from both directions. You must cross the near lane and enter the far lane. Traffic can approach quickly, and on many rural roads visibility might be limited. Even at 55 kilometers an hour, vehicles are closing on you at 15 meters per second. If you look left, turn and look right then pull out, all within three seconds, something that was not within 45 meters before is now upon you.

Remember three things when you pull out:

1. Keep looking in both directions – left and right, left and right, left and right – until you have pulled out.

CLEAR THE WAY

2. If one side has less visibility than the other, concentrate your scanning on that side, but do not neglect the other.
3. As soon as you are in the lane, check your rearview mirror to see what traffic behind you is doing.

STEP SIX: Getting Up to Highway Speeds

[For the Instructor]

This is a variation of Step Five, except that it should take place on uncrowded four-lane highways and on cross-country two-lane arteries, in that order. This is the time to introduce the student to highway speeds – within certain limits.

Top speed for these lessons is 80 kilometers an hour, which should remain the maximum for the student during the first six months of driving.

Even if you conduct the lesson in a rural area on an uncrowded highway with a higher speed limit, do not allow the student to drive faster than 80. Keep in mind that 80 kilometers an hour translates into nearly 25 meters per second. Stopping distance – reaction time plus braking distance – is over 60 meters.

That is a large CLEAR ZONE to maintain, and it takes experience to do so. Despite the drills and practices, novice drivers do not possess sufficient skills and judgment to go any faster safely. Impose 80 as the limit.

Easing onto Highways

When you find an appropriate stretch of highway, spend at least several sessions cruising it, practicing all of the same drills contained in Step Five. A suitable stretch of four-lane highway should not present many roadside hazards, so the student can work on holding a good line and maintaining a steady speed.

You will also need to cover the following new situations:
- Entering and exiting the highway
- Merging with other vehicles
- Passing other vehicles
- Being passed by trucks
- Emergency stopping and reentering highways

Merging

Merging properly onto a highway can be challenging. It requires good judgment and will test the student's ability. You want the student to use the approach ramp and merge lane to accelerate until the vehicle is traveling at or near the same speed as the traffic already on the highway. She must also be able to find an open space in the traffic and move into the lane. It is the correct procedure even if the highway is empty at that moment.

This is a difficult maneuver when done in traffic, which is why you need to find a lightly traveled road. When you find a likely route, select a pair of exits only a few kilometers apart. Then travel back and forth between them, entering and exiting repeatedly.

The goals at the entrance are first to observe and clear the ramp, accelerate smoothly up to the speed of the highway, and then signal and merge into the lane. A lightly traveled road allows room for errors.

You might want to wait on the shoulder until the ramp is empty. Trying to merge in traffic could make the student timid about the maneuver. Use an empty ramp at first to build her confidence. At an exit ramp, she should turn her signals on about 10 seconds before the exit. This likewise should be done whether or not anybody else is on the road. You want it to become a habit.

It is also important to maintain speed until the student has entered the deceleration lane or the ramp itself. Teach her to avoid slowing down until she clears the traffic lane.

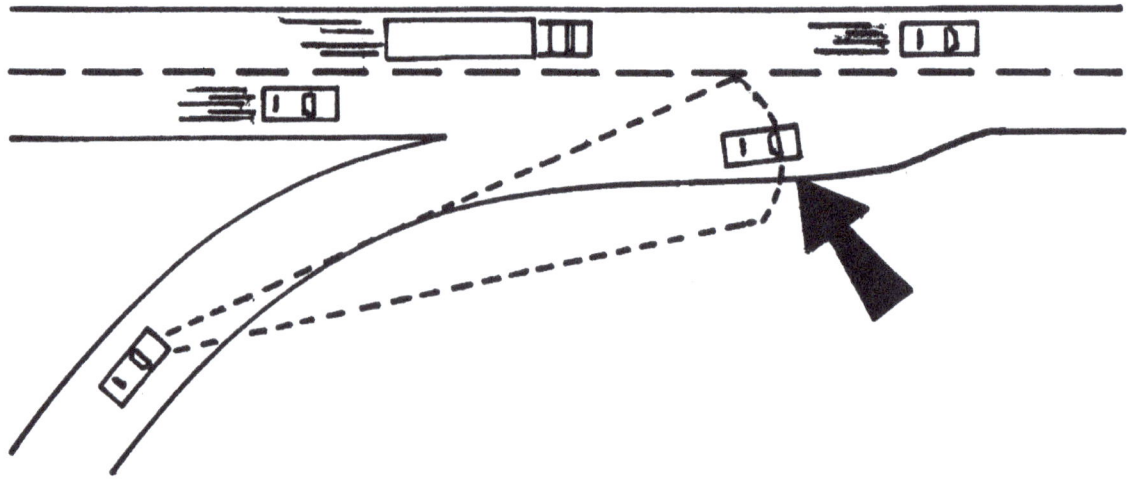

Clear the Ramp First

[For the Student]

The three keys to safe merging:
1. CLEAR THE WAY. Determine how much room there is ahead – on the ramp or the acceleration lane – before you have to move over.
2. Select your place in traffic ahead of time. That means you must examine oncoming traffic, and judge its speed and distance, before moving onto the roadway.
3. Slip into traffic as close as possible to the prevailing speed, not too fast or too slow.

Your place in traffic is like a moving target. Call it your merge slot. It is a large, imaginary space that is already moving with traffic at the proper speed. When you have identified it, and have maneuvered the vehicle into it, you have safely joined the traffic.

Look for the merge slot by looking to the side and glancing at your rearview mirrors. If the highway is empty, pick out an imaginary space anyway, for practice.

Concentrate on the ramp ahead first. This is important! If you focus your attention on the highway or on oncoming traffic you could ignore a hazard sitting on the ramp. Or, the ramp might end suddenly with no merge area. Usually there is a road sign to tell you this, but not always. Whatever, it is critical that you CLEAR THE WAY on the ramp before moving onto the highway.

Never stop on an entrance ramp unless you have no choice. Why would you have no choice?

- There could be a stop sign or road construction.
- Someone could have stopped ahead of you because they never found a merge slot.

Stopping on a ramp is dangerous. For one thing, someone could roll up from behind without looking and crash into you. For another, everyone who stops will have to wait longer to merge. If they attempt to accelerate into traffic from a standing start, the other vehicles must move over or slow down to let them in.

The worst situation is if you attempt to merge from a stop ahead of an oncoming truck. You could misjudge the truck's ability to slow down or stop. Trucks require longer stopping distances than smaller vehicles.

You cannot approach a highway and expect other vehicles to let you in, but if you merge properly – with steady acceleration, no abrupt swerves, no stomping on the gas or hitting the brakes – it should go smoothly. Give yourself as much room as possible and glide into the lane.

Signal until you complete the merge.

Later, when you attempt to merge into heavy traffic, you will know you did it correctly if you have done it smoothly. This could be difficult for a while, so keep trying until you feel confident about it. You cannot practice merging too much.

Remember to **CLEAR THE WAY**. Always pay attention to what is going on in front of you before you attempt to change lanes onto the highway.

Exiting

When you exit, signal your intention at least 10 seconds ahead of time. If you do not know exactly where the exit is – for example, if it is located on the other side of the crest of a hill – then begin signaling as soon as you see the exit sign or the ramp.

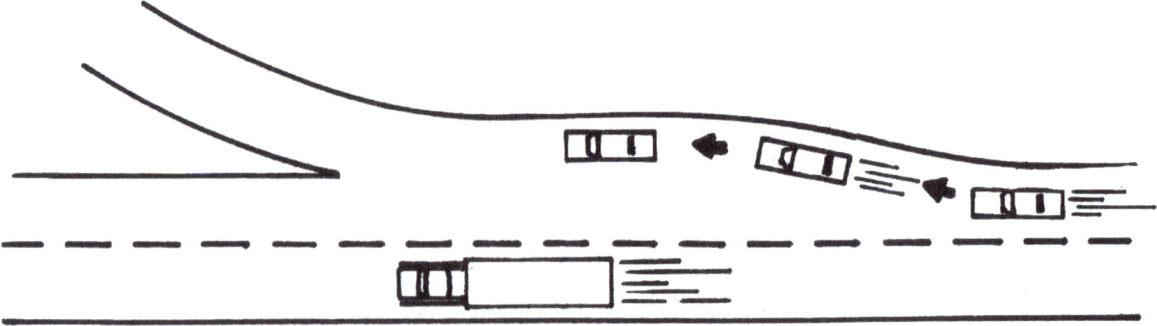

Be predictable. Signal so that drivers behind you will know what you are going to do. When you reach the exit ramp, move over before you slow down. This also is important. Avoid slowing down on the highway. Slow down on the ramp. Many highway crashes happen at entrances and exits. They are places where vehicle speeds and headings can vary greatly. You can reduce your chances of a crash by joining and leaving highway traffic smoothly and at proper speed.

Accelerate and decelerate on the ramps – not on the highway – as much as possible.

Be Courteous to Merging and Exiting Vehicles
It is easier when the situation is reversed. If you are on the highway and encounter traffic entering and exiting, the best thing to do is be courteous and helpful to other drivers. SHARE THE ROAD

If you see a vehicle ahead on an entrance ramp, ease off the gas. Coast and wait for the vehicle to merge. If the driver seems hesitant, flash your headlights quickly. If the driver does not respond, or if the driver appears indecisive, move into the left lane if clear and pass with caution.

- Your best option is to coast behind the vehicle.
- Next is to move left temporarily.
- Last is to pass.

Remember earlier when I described how you can tell if another vehicle is about to intrude into your CLEAR ZONE? The same practice applies here: Watch the vehicle's front wheel. If it begins to turn toward your lane, ease off the gas or, if the adjoining lane is clear, move over.

When a vehicle ahead of you signals to exit, ease off the gas and coast until it moves out of traffic. Your courtesy will go a long way toward allowing other drivers easy merges or exits. The roadway becomes safer because of your actions. Be courteous, but do not depend on the courtesy of others.

Appreciate good manners when they are displayed, but do not assume they will be offered. Take the precautions you can to protect yourself. Make courtesy mandatory for you, but consider it a bonus from others on the road.

Keeping to the Right

[For the Instructor]

A common mistake for drivers, novice and veteran, is to linger in the left lane. Do not allow the student to fall into this habit. The left lane is supposed to be for passing or faster traffic.

You should know from experience that many drivers become angry and rude if someone is blocking the left lane. They are likely to be as impatient with a beginning driver as anyone else, so have the student keep to the right and stay out of their way.

Stay Right, Stay Safe

[For the Student]

Even if the roadway is lightly traveled, get into the habit of staying in the right lane, using the left lanes only for passing. This rule applies to this stage of your instruction and development. Later on, we will discuss an important exception.

If traffic is heavy (which we will cover in Step Nine), it will fill both or all lanes. But whatever the conditions, stay to the right. Do not try to keep up with faster traffic and stay out of its way.

Four-Lane Passing
Passing on a four-lane highway is relatively easy and safe – as long as you avoid being surprised by someone who has been driving in one of your blind spots. As I mentioned earlier, every vehicle has blind spots. They are spaces to the side and behind that are not covered by the mirrors. Someone could be traveling near you in one of your blind spots at any time. The way to overcome this hazard is to CLEAR THE WAY. Look quickly to the side to make sure no one is there and check your mirrors as well.

Whenever you see a slower-moving vehicle ahead, and if the left lane is clear, signal and move over. Pass the slower vehicle but do not pull back to the right, yet. Wait until you can see both headlights of the vehicle in your rearview mirror (not the side mirror). Then signal and return to the right lane. You want to avoid crowding the other driver's **CLEAR ZONE**.

If the left lane is occupied, continue to approach the slower vehicle until you are about three seconds behind it. Remember, you can tell this by taking any landmark, such as a road sign, and counting the seconds from the moment the vehicle ahead passes it until the moment you do. Ease up and stay at that distance until the left lane is clear. Then signal, accelerate and pass. Again, pull back into the right lane only when you can see both headlights.

More About Blind Spots
As much as you need to look out for other vehicles in your blind spots, try likewise to avoid sitting in someone else's. How can you tell? If you can see the other driver's face in their side mirror, then they can see you. If you cannot, the driver might not know you are there.

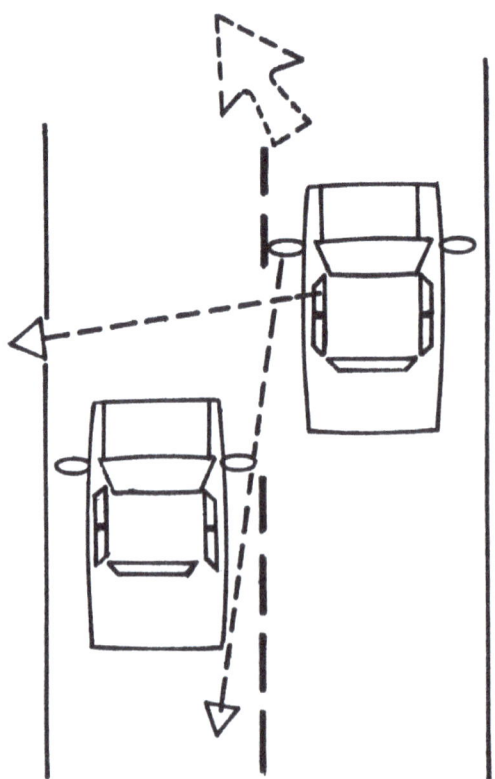

Also, if you are traveling at the same speed as a nearby vehicle and your front fender is beside their rear fender, either to the right or left, you probably are sitting in a blind spot. Whenever this happens, try to move ahead or behind as soon as possible so you can be seen.

Being Passed
You need to know two things when trucks pass you:
1. Be aware that big trucks create bow shocks. These are wide areas of air turbulence. When they pass you, if they are moving 10 to 15 kilometers an hour faster than you are, expect to feel a sudden push away from them. Hold your steering wheel firmly and correct your heading if necessary.
2. When the truck has passed you completely, and is one or two truck-lengths ahead, flash your headlights quickly several times. This is a universal all-clear gesture. It informs truck drivers it is safe to move back into your lane. It makes things easier for them. Many will express thanks by flashing their running lights.

For you, it is another way to SHARE THE ROAD

Hold the Line
When you are not merging, passing or being passed, work on maintaining a good line on the road. Stay in the middle of the lane and avoid weaving. You should know the best way to do this by now: Keep your eyes several seconds ahead or, on curves, on the inside edge of visibility. But most times avoid looking directly at the pavement in front of you. It creates too much visual activity and will tire your eyes quickly. Use your peripheral vision to scan the pavement for hazards.

After you have been driving a while, you will develop a sense of where your vehicle is positioned in the lane. It will become instinctive. The best way to foster this sense is to keep your focus well ahead of where you are – about 100 meters.

Try also to maintain a steady speed. It will help a lot if you are calm and relaxed. The more you drive, the more you will develop a reliable sense of how fast you are going. For now, check your speedometer once or twice each minute. Just glance down at it.

Do Not Take 80 Lightly
In your country, with speed limits so high and many of your drivers willing to exceed them, staying at 80 kilometers an hour might seem unwise or as though you are driving too slowly. Believe me, at this stage of your instruction you are not. When you drive 80, you are already driving beyond the

limit of your vehicle's ability to protect you in a crash — airbags or not. If you hit something at 80, your chances of survival are not good.

Never take speed lightly.
If you have any doubt about how fast you are really going, take a moment sometime when you are doing 80 to observe a passing object such as a bridge abutment or utility pole. Now imagine hitting it. All of a sudden, 80 is not so slow, is it?

Emergency Stopping

[For the Instructor]

While you are cruising along a lightly traveled highway, it might be a good time to introduce the student to the emergency stop. It can be an extremely important and useful maneuver, and it is relatively easy to learn, because it is similar to handling a drop-off. Wait until the highway behind you is clear then have the student practice. Try it several times during the highway lessons, whenever it will not interfere with other vehicles.

Remember to have the student signal before pulling off and stopping.

Stopping Safely in an Emergency

[For the Student]

Stopping properly in an emergency is like handling a drop-off and an exit — except that you are usually not lucky enough to do it on an exit ramp.

The key to a safe emergency stop is to slow down as gradually as possible and give traffic behind you as much warning of your intentions as you can.

Here are the steps:
1. Ease off the gas. (Have you noticed how many times this is the best first thing to do?)
2. Turn your signals on.
3. Make sure the shoulder of the road ahead is well clear of obstacles.
4. Move over to the far edge of the pavement.

5. Continue coasting until your speed drops to about 70.
6. Gradually steer off the roadway and onto the shoulder.
7. Gently brake to a crawl.
8. Pull as far away from the road as possible, at least the width of a lane.
9. If you must remain near the roadway, turn your emergency flashers on.

It is important to make this a gradual maneuver. Sudden swerves can throw the vehicle out of control. If you are driving a sport-utility vehicle, it could even roll over.

One possible reason for an emergency stop is a flat tire or a sudden loss of tire pressure called a blow-out. If you ever experience this, it can be frightening. Your first impulse might be to slam on the brakes.

In two words: Do not!

When one tire goes flat, it creates a severe drag on the other wheels. If you hit the brakes – even with an antilock braking system – you will add to the instability of the situation. The best thing to do is steer your way off the highway. Hold a straight line and resist the temptation to brake. Bring the vehicle to a gentle stop using the steps listed above.

Returning Safely to the Road
Make this maneuver as close to a merge as possible. Judge how much room there is ahead on the shoulder before you return to the pavement. If there is plenty of room:
1. Turn your flashers off and your turn signals on.
2. Get rolling only if there is a break in traffic.
3. Stay on the shoulder until your speed is at least 70.
4. Move over as soon as possible – but do not swerve – and quickly accelerate to your normal speed.
5. Turn your signal off.

If there is no room to make a rolling start, you will have to watch for a big traffic opening, because you will have to do all of your accelerating on the highway. Put your signal on and wait for a clearing. Keep watching the rearview mirror to see if someone behind you flashes their headlights or moves over to let you in. If they do, take advantage quickly.

Remember to be courteous to other drivers in this situation. If they are signaling an emergency stop, ease up until they have moved off the road. If they have stopped too near the traffic lane, ease off the gas or move over if the adjacent lane is clear until you pass them. If they are trying to get back on the road, ease up and flash them in or move out of the lane if you can. SHARE THE ROAD

Resuming Practice on Two-Lane Roads

[For the Instructor]

If the student has mastered the basics of merging, exiting, passing and being passed, and if you think she can maintain her speed and a good line on a four-lane highway, then it is probably time to move back to two-lane blacktop. Only this time, find a cross-country artery with a bit of traffic, both automobiles and trucks as well as some stoplights, side roads, driveways, curves and hills.

Now have the student repeat all of the drills in Step Five; except remember that the CLEAR ZONE is at least 75 meters. Many circumstances along the road will not provide that much visibility; these maneuvers will require a lot of varying speed.

You Will Need Two Sets of Eyes
Your co-piloting will be even more important here. Two-lane roads are, mile for mile, the most dangerous highways. It is easy to understand why. When drivers pass, they must do so into the oncoming traffic lane. At 80 to 85 kilometers an hour, that is a combined speed of up to 170 whenever two vehicles approach each other. When someone behaves impulsively or misjudges how much room they have, the results can be devastating.

High-speed head-ons have high fatality rates, so be extremely careful. **Have the student practice the following new situations:**
- Pulling off and pulling onto high-speed two-lane highways
- Encountering other vehicles pulling on and off
- Following at a safe distance
- Dealing with tailgaters
- Being passed

Notice that I did not include passing here. That is because passing on a two-lane highway is too dangerous for learning drivers to attempt. I am not talking about passing a farm tractor or a heavily loaded truck that is straining along at 40 kilometers an hour, although even those situations call for great care. No. It takes strong skills and sharp judgment to overtake another vehicle on two lanes with oncoming traffic. Save it for later, after the license has been obtained.

One more thing: I recommend using low-beam headlights at all times on roads like these. For many vehicles, that means turning them on manually.

Enter With Caution

[For the Student]

Pulling onto a high-speed two-lane highway requires even more caution than normal. You have to be sure not only that there is no immediate oncoming traffic but also that you get up to speed quickly. Otherwise someone could be roaring up behind you.

As with other complex maneuvers, it will take time for you to develop a good sense of when to move. It is best when starting out to "err on the side of caution," as they say. In other words, give yourself lots of room. If you have any doubts, wait. If there are others behind you and they seem to be growing impatient, wave them around you. Do not let yourself be pressured into taking risks.

Whenever you begin a maneuver, if you are out on the highway and in the lane, do not delay getting up to speed. That does not mean you need to "floor" the gas pedal. Just do not dawdle.

Highway Turnoffs
Turning safely from a highway with no exit ramps requires one critical ingredient: predictability. The traffic behind you must know for sure what you are about to do.
- Put your signals on at least 10 seconds ahead of the turn.
- Ease off the gas pedal.
- Begin to brake gently.
- Slow down enough to make the turn safely.
- Make the turn.

The more predictably you perform, the safer this maneuver will be. Pay attention so you will not have to make any abrupt moves.

Other Highway Encounters
If you follow the rules, then encountering another vehicle pulling out or turning off should not be a problem. If you see someone pulling out ahead, ease off the gas. Coast until the other vehicle reaches cruising speed. SHARE THE ROAD

The same with a vehicle pulling off of the highway: As soon as you see the turn signal, ease off the gas. Coast or brake gently until it leaves the road. Either way, your CLEAR ZONE should keep you safely behind until the other vehicle joins or leaves traffic.
If a vehicle overtakes you or moves out to pass in a two-lane situation, as soon as you notice it, ease off the gas until the vehicle returns to the lane in front of you. This is one of the most helpful and important ways to **SHARE THE ROAD**. Anytime you follow another vehicle on a two-lane highway, you must be extra careful. Allow yourself enough room to stop if that vehicle stops or pulls off suddenly – because you do not want to be forced into the oncoming lane.

Do not rely on other drivers to use their turn signals. Some people never signal properly. Or, they will suddenly turn off the highway because they have misjudged where the turn is. So, always be aware of the distance between you and the vehicle ahead. If that distance begins to shorten, whether or not you see signals or even brake lights, react accordingly. Your safe following distance should be based on the Three-Second Rule: Whatever the speed, it should take at least three seconds for you to reach the same spot as the vehicle in front of you. That is a minimum distance. Never follow another vehicle more closely than that.

Remember also how to calculate it: As soon as the front vehicle crosses a landmark – a road sign or a tree or an overpass – begin counting: "one-one thousand, two-one thousand, three-one thousand…." If you can count through "three-one thousand," you are far enough behind.

Many drivers fail to maintain a safe following distance. Many drivers also speed. Chances are, if you are traveling on a two-lane highway (and chances are, there will not be Saher cameras monitoring the traffic), other vehicles will begin to pull up close behind you. When this happens, do not be nervous. **Do as follows:**
- Maintain your speed. Do not slow down or speed up. Be consistent and predictable.

- If there is no traffic ahead of you, and the roadway is generally clear of hazards, the vehicle behind you will take the first opportunity to pass.

Most major two-lane roads have a double yellow line down the middle. Passing zones either feature a single broken line, or a solid line left/broken line right combination. As soon as you reach a passing zone, and the left lane is free of oncoming traffic, ease off the gas and let the tailing vehicle pass.

If you have traffic ahead, or if there are curves or hills or hazards on the road, continue to maintain your CLEAR ZONE. If the vehicle behind is following too closely, do one of two things:
1. Look for the first opportunity to pull over, put your turn signal on, and ease out of the lane until you are passed.
2. If there is nowhere to pull over, and the tailgater persists, put your emergency flashers on until they back off. If this does not work, ease off the gas and move as far right as possible until the vehicle passes.

Never hit your brakes in an effort to frustrate a tailgater. It is a dangerous thing to do. It could cause a collision or trigger an angry confrontation. Never try to correct another driver. If people are behaving unsafely, avoid them.

If you see one vehicle passing another in the distance and approaching you, take your foot off the gas. Ease up until the passing vehicle is back in the oncoming lane. Make sure your low-beams are on to maximize your visibility to oncoming traffic.

Two-Lane Passing
Which brings us to passing. My advice is not to try it – not yet. You are not ready for this maneuver. Passing another vehicle on a major two-lane road requires fully developed skills. The closing speed between two vehicles, each traveling 80 kilometers an hour, is nearly 45 meters per second. You are going to need about 10 seconds to pass another vehicle, which means you need a minimum of 450 meters. That is nearly half a kilometer!

LEARN THE LIMITS

Do not attempt to pass unless you encounter a slow-moving vehicle, and only then if you are absolutely sure the way ahead is clear. Also make sure you can pass before the passing zone ends. If so, do all of the following:

1. Make sure passing is permitted. The road will have either a broken center line or a combination with the broken line on the right.
2. Check your blind spot in case someone behind you has moved out to pass.
3. Make sure the vehicle in front of you is not about to make a turn – particularly a left turn.
4. Signal as soon as you make the decision.
5. Accelerate strongly until you are out in front of the next vehicle. On a two-lane road, you should be going at least 15 kilometers an hour faster than it is.
6. Do not move back until you can see both headlights in the rearview mirror.
7. Do not slow down until you are back in the right lane.
8. Do not swerve. Signal and move over quickly but smoothly.
9. Ease back to your cruising speed.
10. If for some reason (oncoming traffic has appeared, for example) you decide not to pass, signal and ease back behind the other vehicle. Never try to force your way in front of it.
11. Again, do not pass unless you are absolutely sure it is safe.

Do not pass another vehicle at all if it is moving close to the speed limit. Wait until you have been driving at least six months before you attempt this maneuver on anything but a slow-moving vehicle.

STEP SEVEN: Night Driving

[For the Instructor]

Night driving is different from daytime driving, for obvious reasons, but the same skills apply to both.

The variations include:
- Learning when to turn headlights on
- Learning when to use high and low beams
- Avoiding "overdriving" headlights
- Dealing with headlights from oncoming and overtaking vehicles
- Noticing reflections, contrast, and movement

For Step Seven, you should use the same locations that were visited in Steps Three through Six. Return to the places you used in daylight and let the student practice at dusk and at night.

You can skip the beginning parking lot and the back streets. Start with the neighborhood roads, move to the commercial strip then on to the country roads, lightly-traveled highways, and main two-lane roads.

Lights On

[For the Student]

Many drivers delay too long turning their headlights on. They figure that if they still can see the road well, there is no reason to turn the lights on. But headlights have two purposes: Not only do they help you see when it is dark, but they also help other drivers see you.

You should follow three rules regarding headlights:
1. Turn your low-beams on as soon as the sun goes down. (Sometimes this is called "the magic hour.")
2. Turn them on if the daytime weather is heavily overcast, rainy, snowy or foggy.
3. Turn them on anytime you are traveling a two-lane road.

It is true that most modern vehicles feature automatic headlights or even separate daytime driving lights. Then why am I discussing this? Because in my experience many automatic settings fail to activate the headlights for too long when daylight begins to dim or when clouds darken the sky. In fact, from my direct observation I have found that this deficiency affects almost two in ten vehicles. Therefore, I recommend turning the lights on at the first hint that daylight has begun to dim.

You need to illuminate yourself as well as the road ahead.

Low-Beams
Low-beams are aimed low and to the right. They are meant to accommodate both you and oncoming drivers while you are passing each other. They also should be used if you see a pedestrian walking in your direction. Even if someone is on a sidewalk, if she is facing you, your
high-beams can be blinding.

In heavy traffic, use low-beams only.

High-Beams
High-beams are aimed higher and more toward the center of the road. They are designed to give you maximum visibility, but they also can be blinding to other drivers. As soon as you see headlights approaching you, dim your lights. The same when you approach drivers ahead. Your high-beams become an annoyance if they are shining in their review mirror, so dim them as soon as they begin to illuminate the back of another vehicle.

If an oncoming driver fails to dim, flash your high-beams briefly. If you are ignored, do not put your high-beams back on. Keep your eyes lowered and to the right of the roadway until the other vehicle passes.

Flash your high-beams at trucks and trailers if they pass you as soon as there is room for them to pull back into the right lane. This is a particularly valuable courtesy at night.

Headlight Limits
It is possible to "overdrive" your headlights. That is, you can be going fast enough that your stopping distance is farther than your headlights allow you to see. If an unexpected hazard appears, you might not be able to stop in time.

If you stay at 80 and under, this usually is not a problem on a straight road. On hills and curves, you should be using your CLEAR ZONE to govern your speed anyway, just as you would in daytime.

'Ice Cream'
Here is a good general strategy for driving at night. It involves three components that almost always indicate a hazard or cause for attention: contrast, reflection and movement. They are the inconsistencies I discussed in Step Four.

Inconsistencies: contrast, reflection and movement.
I = C.R.M.
Think "ice cream."

If you pick up inconsistencies early, you can deal with them. Everything is sweet, like ice cream. But if you miss something and a hazard appears in front of you suddenly, you might be thinking something else: "I scream!"

Anything that reflects your headlights brightly should attract your attention:
- The reflective surface of a road sign, which you will want to read
- A piece of glass or metal on or beside the road, which you want to avoid
- Reflective striping on a cyclist or pedestrian
- The eyes of a wild animal

In all of these cases, reflections are something to be noticed. Likewise, contrast could indicate a pothole, or something lying in the road. Movement always should attract your attention immediately. As you drive at night, the passing road and landscape take on a particular pattern. As long as the pattern remains consistent, you can relax and proceed at a steady rate. But whenever something appears that is inconsistent – contrast, reflection or movement – you should instantly raise your attention level. Focus on that inconsistency until you identify it and decide how to react to it. Most of the time, you will not have to react at all, but you never want to ignore an inconsistency.

STEP EIGHT: City Streets

[For the Instructor]

This is a variation of Steps Three and Four, involving heavy, slow-moving traffic in stop-and-go situations; except that in urban areas, you have the added complication of narrow lanes, many more pedestrians and spillovers at intersections.

There is not much new to learn here in terms of rules or special skills, but streets are more challenging than parking lots. It is important to expose the student to dense city traffic, but you also should wait until she has gained some overall experience. Hence, city driving follows country highway driving.

You will need to watch out for the following situations:
- Tight lane squeezes
- Crowding from trucks and buses
- Doors suddenly opening on parked vehicles
- Spillover traffic at intersections

- Drivers trying to turn through clogged lanes
- Uneven pavement and sudden changes in street conditions
- One-way streets

Continue co-piloting and spend at least a half-dozen sessions in city traffic. Concentrate on getting the student to THINK AHEAD. It is the fourth of the five themes – making the correct decisions ahead of time to avoid awkward maneuvers and situations.

Make sure the student gains some experience dealing with one-way streets, both driving on them and turning onto them. Make sure she recognizes "ONE WAY" and "DO NOT ENTER" signs. Do not take it for granted; all of this is still new.

While you are in the city, it is finally time to try parallel parking. The student has been driving long enough now that this should not present a major challenge. When I began teaching my daughters, they both seemed quite worried about the prospect of parallel parking, so I postponed it until late in the instruction. Then I told them something that erased their anxiety: How difficult can anything be that you do at one kilometer an hour?

Steady, Straight and Calm

[For the Student]

City driving can rattle even the most experienced of us. The volume of activity, coupled with the tension and quick tempers that many people naturally display in this environment, can create unpleasant and frustrating experiences.

By now, you have been exposed to most of the basic situations you will encounter – though in greater numbers and frequency – in the city. You should know, for example, that when you are traveling in traffic in a narrow lane, you must focus ahead to help you hold a steady line. This will be particularly useful when you are traveling beside a city bus or a large truck.

You also should know to CLEAR THE WAY ahead, so if you are passing by a long line of parallel-parked cars, you should be constantly noticing whether any of them is about to pull out, or whether someone is inside who might open a door suddenly.

Theme Four of Five: THINK AHEAD

There is also something new to learn here. It is the fourth of the five themes: THINK AHEAD. It sounds simple. It is. It is also important in tight traffic situations. It means always try to keep in mind what you need to do well ahead of time so you can avoid sudden moves, interference with others or inconvenient mistakes.

Examples:

- You need to make a left turn ahead, but you are in the wrong lane. Solution: Do not wait. Signal and move over as soon as an opening appears.

- Even though traffic ahead is jammed up, you continue to move forward into an intersection. You get stuck there when the light changes and now you are blocking cross traffic. Solution: Make sure there is enough room for you to get through an intersection before you enter. If not, wait behind the stop line for a space to clear.

- You are stopped at a stop light in front of an alley or parking lot entrance. An oncoming vehicle wants to turn left into that space but cannot because you are blocking it. Solution: Any time you see a traffic clog or a stop light ahead, make sure you do not block an entrance.

An exit is another story. It is nice to leave an exit open, but not necessary. If there is room, allow a waiting vehicle to pull out in front of you as soon as traffic ahead begins moving.
In these examples, you need to **THINK AHEAD**. Try to recognize such situations before they develop. As long as you do, you can be the best possible city driver: steady, straight and calm. You become invisible in the sea of vehicles, because you are not making any sudden movements, and you are not holding up anybody else.

Parallel Parking

Sooner or later, you are going to have to parallel park. A lot of students seem to consider this the ultimate driving challenge. It really does not amount to much. Think about it. How difficult could it be if you are moving much more slowly than you can walk?

Here are the basics:
1. When you see a space, slow down, put your turn signal on and pull beside the vehicle parked ahead of the space.
2. Make sure the traffic behind you is stopped or pulling around before you begin backing up.
3. Divide the space into imaginary thirds. Using the back end of your vehicle as a reference, steer it into the space at the two-thirds mark at about a 45-degree angle.
4. When your back end is mostly inside the space, begin to straighten out but keep an eye on the front vehicle to avoid scraping it with your fender.
5. Keep backing up until your back end is nearly touching the vehicle behind you, straightening out as much as possible.
6. Pull up so you end up in the center of the space.

That is it!

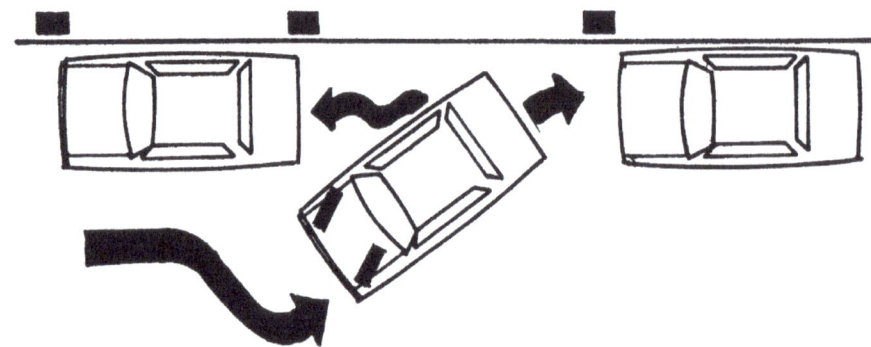

Back up very slowly at first. It will help you position the vehicle properly. Remember to turn the steering wheel only when you are moving, unless the space is so tight there is no choice.

If you have parked well, the vehicle should end up about 15 centimeters from the curb. Farther away and you risk sticking out into the street where you could be sideswiped. Closer in and it becomes difficult to pull out. Also, you could scrape your tires and wheel covers on the curb.

Practice Makes Perfect

[For the Instructor]

Be patient through this. It could take several tries before the student gets it right. You might want to begin on a quiet side street, so she can practice the maneuver without worrying about traffic. Do it on both sides of the street. Start on the right side, of course, but as soon as the student begins to handle it well, find a one-way street with parallel parking and work on pulling into a space on the left side.

STEP NINE: Into Heavy Traffic

[For the Instructor]

These next two steps are the most difficult in the series by far. They introduce the student to the most complex situations on the highways: in this case, heavy traffic at high speeds. It is where impatience, lack of skill and emotional outbursts often combine to produce continually hazardous conditions. Everyone is at risk here, no matter how competent. Even if the previous steps have gone well, you might want to postpone Step Nine until the student has obtained her license and has been driving for several more months.

Driving on urban highways and other heavy traffic situations is different from anything else the student has experienced so far. It requires a combination of a high level of attention and strong skills to keep safe. Again, it is not thinking that is needed so much as heightened senses and proper attitude. The driver must be constantly alert but relaxed at the same time. Too much thinking in this situation causes fatigue, and fatigue lowers reaction time and causes accidents. There is a vast difference between being inattentive and preoccupied and being a detached and relaxed driver.

If you decide to attempt these lessons, spend as much time as you can in heavy highway traffic. But even after the license, advise the student not to attempt this environment alone for a while. She has not been driving enough for all of her necessary reflexes to develop.

Heavy-Traffic Skills
In this step, the student needs to practice all of the components taught in the other steps; the main difference is the conditions will be much more challenging.

The components include:
- Merging into and exiting the traffic flow
- Maintaining a good line
- Choosing and changing lanes

- Passing
- Maintaining proper following distance
- Accelerating and braking within traffic

There also are three new items:
- Predicting and reacting to the pack behavior of drivers
- Detecting traffic clogs ahead
- Maneuvering through narrow lanes in construction zones

You need to take extreme care for every one of these situations. If you have any doubts, postpone this step. Do not subject an inexperienced driver to heavy, high-speed traffic until she is ready.

When you think the time is right, find a major traffic artery and map out a course along it. Where I live, outside Washington, D.C., we have a notorious highway called the Beltway. It is an oppressively trafficked, eight-lane highway circling some 100 kilometers around the city. It takes about an hour and a quarter to complete one loop – assuming that traffic hasn't become snarled or stopped by a crash. An hour and a quarter is about the right duration for these lessons.

If you do not have a similar roadway, pick a stretch of about 50 kilometers along any heavily traveled expressway and follow it in both directions. You and the student will have to make dozens of trips along the route before basic competence begins to appear.

Approaching Heavy Traffic

[For the Student]

You can approach driving in heavy highway traffic in three ways. First is to drive aggressively, with little regard for others on the road. Aggressive drivers move at excessive speed at every opportunity. They challenge other drivers as soon as they enter the highway, and they perpetrate a dangerous practice I call "slicing," meaning they will suddenly cut across multiple lanes when they exit. They also weave in and out of lanes, always striving to get in front. It is an extremely unsafe approach. It endangers everyone nearby, and it can even elicit copycat reactions in other drivers. The huge toll in life and limb that aggression and speed take on the roads each year is testimony to the folly of such habits.

The second approach is what I see being followed by most people on today's highways, whether in my country or yours – the Saher system notwithstanding. It is a form of pack mentality. There is a euphemism in the United States that you might have heard as well. It is called "keeping up with traffic." It means no matter what the legal speed limit is, drivers should go with the flow.

But pack driving is unsafe, because the tone of the packs is aggressive. Everyone is trying to push through the group. As a result, the general speed increases and distances diminish among vehicles. Sooner or later, someone makes a misjudgment, and things quickly go wrong. At the least, it becomes an annoyance for everyone else, because the crashes resulting from misjudgments stop traffic or slow it to a crawl through a bottleneck until the wreckage is cleared. Some of the worst pile-ups in history have resulted from packs, particularly when visibility is low, or the road surface is slippery, or both.

Going Against the Crowd

The third approach is the one I practice and recommend. It does not involve driving too slowly, which can also be dangerous because it elicits frustration and anger in other drivers. I have a name for my preferred method. I call it "driving backwards."

I agree it is an odd-sounding term. But it is also a way to drive in traffic without participating in the packs or becoming caught up in the pressures. The technique is safe, simple and straightforward, and it can work for you whether you are a beginner or have accumulated many years behind the wheel. It involves doing one of two things: driving the speed limit or driving slightly slower than the pack, whichever is slower. Please bear with me.

Relativity Is the Key

The key to safe driving in traffic is not the particular speed of your vehicle but its relative speed, along with the distance you maintain between your vehicle and everyone else's. For example, if you are driving 60 kilometers an hour but are surrounded closely by other vehicles moving at 100, you are creating a hazard for everyone else because you are forcing other drivers to maneuver around you at high speed. Conversely, if you drive 100 and everyone else is going 60 on a packed highway, you likewise create a hazard by requiring yourself to maneuver among the other vehicles. In both cases, the slightest miscalculation will cause a crash.

But what if those two speed comparisons occurred on a highway where many meters separated every vehicle? In such cases the level of danger would be greatly reduced. Your challenge on crowded highways, where you do not have the luxury of wide safety margins, is to narrow your speed relative to the traffic around you while increasing the distance between your vehicle and others as much as possible.

That is why I recommended driving backwards, so to speak: Drive at either the speed limit or slightly slower than the speed of surrounding traffic, whichever is lower. Doing so actually solves both challenges. Here is how:

- First, by reducing your speed slightly (less than 5 kilometers an hour) versus surrounding traffic, you will find that the other vehicles will flow past you more or less in orderly fashion. As I stated, in today's heavy-traffic environments, most drivers continually press for advantage versus everyone else – they have grown accustomed to passing other vehicles, so they likely will take little notice of your moving a little more slowly.
- Second, as you reduce your speed relative to the pack, the other drivers will eventually leave you behind. At a certain point, because there are gaps in the highway packs, you will enjoy an interval of being alone even on the busiest of roads. I know this because I practice it.

Why do I call it "driving backwards?" It has to do with the concept of relativity. In a sense, as other vehicles pass you and then move far ahead of you as a group, you will feel the sensation of backing away – you truly will seem to be moving backwards.

Now, let me return to something I mentioned early in the text. Do you remember when I warned about the need to avoid situations where your survival depends on you reacting instantly and perfectly to a hazard? That is exactly what driving "backwards" in heavy traffic will allow you to do. Keeping your distance from the vehicles in front of you, particularly if they are bunched up tightly and moving in excess of the speed limit, will give you precious extra time to react in case something ugly develops. By continually backing away from densely packed highway traffic, you will create precious extra seconds to detect trouble ahead.

Always Be Predictable

Here is a second, essential safe-driving habit for crowded highways: Behave so that every nearby driver knows not only what you are doing but what you are about to do. In other words, to be safe while moving within traffic, your actions must be completely predictable.

- Make your accelerations and decelerations as gradual as possible.
- Signal well in advance anytime you change lanes or exit.

Everyone on the road needs to feel reasonably certain about what everyone else is doing. As long as this situation prevails, so does safety. But when packs of vehicles increase their speed, with many drivers jockeying to get ahead, predictability disappears very quickly.

The way to remain safe in traffic is to travel at a steady speed, with gradual shifts in lane, acceleration and deceleration. As long as you practice this, use my method of driving "backwards" and avoid blocking the passing lanes, you will have no trouble even in the heaviest traffic.

The Safest Place

You might wonder, if you are driving along a highway with four or more lanes going in the same direction, what is the safest lane to use. You might also think it is the right lane. Well, I once thought that way and advocated remaining in the right lane and allowing all traffic to flow to the left of me. But I no longer agree with my own previous advice. Many more years of observation have changed my mind.

In a heavy-traffic, multilane-highway situation, your safest position is in the center-left lane – or, in the case of more than four unidirectional lanes, next to the far-left lane.

Why did I change my recommendation? It is a reaction to what I have noticed in the lanes to the right. At high speed and in heavy traffic, the right lanes have become dangerously chaotic.

- Drivers enter the highway from the right and immediately accelerate for advantage.
- Drivers exit across multiple lanes at the last possible moment.
- Drivers in the right lanes shift lanes frequently in further attempts to gain advantage.

Compared to the right and entrance/exit lanes, the center-left lane has become an island of sanity. While the far-left lane provides nearly a racetrack environment, with each passing vehicle seemingly going faster than the last, the lane to the right offers relative calm.

I first realized this phenomenon several years ago, when I noticed that truck drivers seemed to stay in the center-right lane and avoided the right lane entirely. It made sense to me. Right lanes on expressways have become crash-prone because of the chaos resulting from so many disorderly attempts at entrances and exits. Then I further noticed that the lane to the left of the truckers offered even less chaos and more predictability. That is when I began using center-left as my preferred lane and it is when I changed my thinking.

Now, I urge you to adopt this tactic and apply it along with driving "backwards" and maintaining your predictability.

Stay Out of the Left Lane
You might ask why you should not stay in the far-left lane, which is even farther away from the chaos and confusion of the exit and merge ramps. It is not a good idea. The fastest and most aggressive drivers – and this applies to the 70 percent of the world that drives on the right side of the road – inhabit the far-left lane. They react most unkindly to anyone who blocks their path by driving more slowly than they do.

Please do not think because you are obeying the speed limit that no one will bother you in the left lane. Worse, do not think that other drivers must be courteous to you even if you are holding them back. And never, never, deliberately do so. It will make other drivers extremely angry.

Many tailgaters erupt into rage if they believe someone is blocking them. This is a serious act that could cause a crash or a violent confrontation.

Tight Merges
Merging into traffic is complicated. You must scan the traffic, pick your entrance spot, move your vehicle into position and avoid running out of ramp.

You can simplify things, however. First, make sure there is a merge ramp, also called an acceleration lane. Some older highways have very short ramps. Some even have none at all. Do not assume you have room to merge – be certain.

Next, determine how much space you have on the ramp. If there is plenty of space, merging becomes a question of getting up to speed, turning your signal on as soon as you become visible to oncoming vehicles, choosing your merge slot and moving into it. Chances are if you are moving at the right speed, someone in the lane will let you in. But be sure the slot is available before you take it.

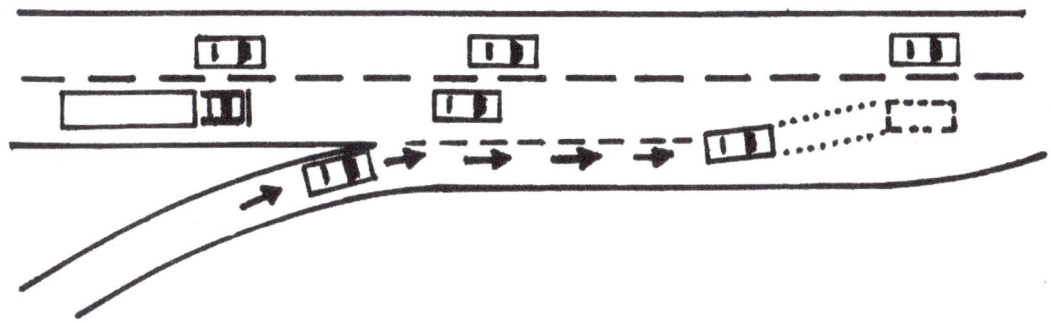

On the other hand, if the merge ramp is short, you must **THINK AHEAD**. You must find your merge slot before you run out of ramp.

What if you cannot find a merge slot? Then cut back your speed early on the ramp until you do see a slot. When you see one, accelerate and move into it. Do not stop. Slow to a crawl if you must, but do not stop.

Worst case: no ramp, no room. Then you have no alternative. Pull up to the stopping place. If traffic is slow, ease in. If it is high speed, you are going to have to wait until you have enough room to move over. If traffic is moving at 90 kilometers an hour, that is 25 meters a second. You will need at least five seconds to merge, or 125 meters of space.

The good news is that worst-case merges are rare. Most of the time, you should be able to find a slot and move into it without causing a disruption of traffic flow or scaring yourself to death. Just remember the rules.

Mixing Loops
Many modern highways now have mixing loops at interchanges. They are exit and entrance lanes forming a loop from an overpass or underpass. Mixing loops can be challenging, because traffic entering and exiting the highway must share the same lane. If you are entering, you must merge with exiting traffic moving faster and trying to cross over into your lane.

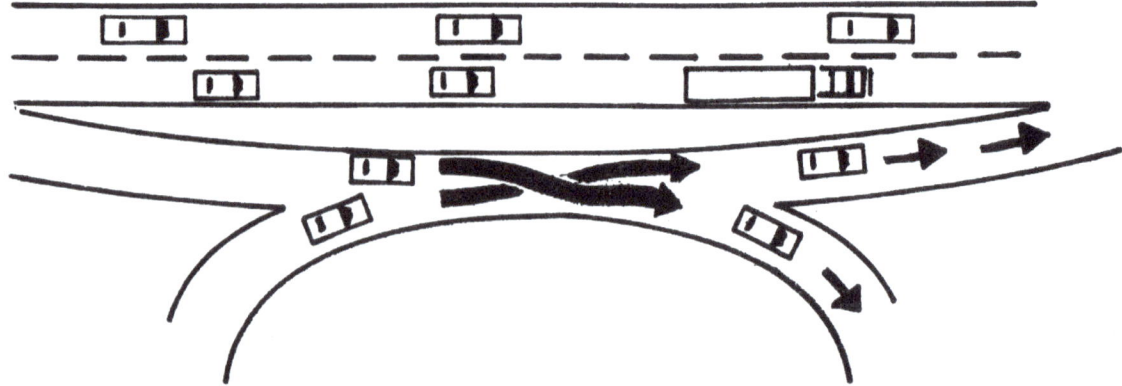

There are no easy rules here, and mixing loops are frequent sites of crashes. So, be careful. Focus your attention on the loop lane until you are parallel to the acceleration/deceleration lane. **Then do one of two things:**

- If exiting traffic is overtaking you, let it cut in front of you.
- If you are in the clear, signal and move over. Exiting traffic should let you cross in front.

Watch out, however, for drivers who use mixing loops to cut ahead of stalled traffic on the highway. They create danger. **When you exit on a mixing loop, use common sense and courtesy:**

- If you overtake a vehicle in the loop, signal and move over in front.
- If the vehicle is beside you or in front of you, ease up and slip in behind it.

Blending
In Step Six, we covered changing lanes, passing, being passed, and maintaining enough stopping distance. Everything is basically the same here, with one important difference: Most of the time, you will be surrounded by other vehicles, all trying to do what you are doing. This is where you must practice predictability and courtesy – and you must blend in with traffic.

SHARE THE ROAD

Blending has two components:

- Reacting properly to what is happening around you
- Whenever possible, allowing others to pass by

If everyone was courteous, the roads would be much, much safer. But courtesy does not seem to be on the minds of many motorists. That does not mean it should not be practiced, however. Simply be aware of what the other drivers around you are trying to do.

- Someone ahead trying to merge? Let them in. If there is room, move over a lane so they can have an easy time finding their merge slot.
- Someone trying to pass? Let them go by. Stay in the right lane when you are not passing or move to the right as soon as you can.
- Someone wants to change lanes? Let them change lanes, even if they are aggressive or driving unsafely. Do not increase tension or add to the problem by getting in their way.

It is that simple, but you will need time to develop a sense of what is going on with the other drivers.

Clogs

A common occurrence on heavily traveled highways is the sudden appearance of clogs. They are clumps of vehicles either crawling along or stopped altogether. Sometimes, clogs are caused by crashes that block one or more lanes. Other times, clogs appear because there are too many vehicles for the amount of pavement available. Whatever, you want to spot clogs as soon as possible because you do not want to be caught in a chain-reaction pile-up. That happens when somebody stops suddenly and is hit from behind by someone who could not react in time and who in turn is hit from behind, and so on.

The best way to spot traffic clogs in sufficient time is to be alert to clusters of brake lights appearing ahead. They mean traffic is slowing down or stopping for some reason. Anytime you see this, ease off the gas and prepare to slow down or stop. Tap your brake pedal gently several times to alert drivers behind you. Activate your emergency flashers if necessary.

As you approach a clog, determine how best to deal with it:

- If the clog is affecting all lanes, slow down as gradually as possible, turning on your emergency flashers if traffic is moving up rapidly behind you.
- If the clog affects only one or a part of the lanes, you likewise need to slow down, because that type of clog creates a danger.

We humans tend to want to avoid confinement, and motorists seem to be the most averse to the condition. When clogs develop, motorists will attempt to jump into lanes that are moving more freely. As long as they do so carefully, it is not a problem. But as you will learn, motorists being careful is a rarity. More common is the sight of vehicles suddenly slipping out of stalled or crawling lanes into the clear – mimicking the behavior seen at highway entrances.

If you are moving along a clear lane next to a clog, moderate your speed in case a vehicle jumps out of the clog and in front of you, and maintain that lower speed until you have passed by the clog completely.

Do Not Pass on the Right
Passing in the right lane has become common on highways, particularly in heavy traffic, but it is usually illegal and often dangerous. Do not fall into the habit. When you need to pass another vehicle, do so to the left.

Watch Out for Weavers and Slicers
It is also common in traffic to encounter lane weavers: drivers who change lanes frequently and rapidly. In a typical situation, you will be overtaken by a vehicle in an adjacent lane being followed by a weaver. As soon as there is enough space between you and the vehicle ahead, the weaver will dart in front of you. This is another illegal and dangerous activity. The best thing to do is stay out of it. If you see a weaver approaching in your mirror, ease off the gas to allow the quickest possible opportunity for that vehicle to get by.

The same goes for slicers, those individuals I mentioned earlier who stay in the left lanes until the last possible moment then suddenly cross whole roadways to exit. I have seen this immature act performed so many times I am sure it is a game some motorists like to play. Unfortunately, sometimes their game ends in smashed metal or worse.

My advice here is the same as for aggressive drivers in the left lane: Stay out of their way. If you notice a slicer approaching in your rearview mirror, ease off the gas and let them go by. Do not interfere with their foolishness.

Better Behind Than Ahead
Another important thing to remember: Whenever you are dealing with aggressive or unsafe drivers, the best place to be is behind them. As long as you are following, you are in a position to react to them and protect yourself. You cannot do much if they are behind you.

Holding Your Line

Moving in heavy traffic, you might find it difficult to hold the vehicle in a steady line. That is what will happen if you limit your attention to the vehicle immediately in front of you.

You need to keep a deeper focus. As much as possible, try to look through the vehicle ahead and pull visual clues from the roadway, the guard rails and the landscape. Remember, your hands will follow your eyes.

Navigating Narrow Lanes

You will eventually encounter another difficult and potentially dangerous situation: shifted and narrow lanes due to construction.

Most construction sites require reduced speeds to help traffic move safely through the disrupted area. But many drivers fail to slow through construction zones, just as they speed everywhere else. This can be highly unnerving in multiple-lane situations.

The key to navigating narrow lanes, as in so many other highway and traffic conditions, is to keep your attention well ahead. But you will have to concentrate even harder to maintain a good line. Try to keep everything else out of your mind while driving through a construction zone. Concentrate on staying in the center of the lane.

Always be extremely careful around highway construction workers. They have one of the most dangerous jobs on earth. Ease off the gas anytime you see them near the roadside. Give them as much room as you can.

STEP TEN: Harsh Weather

[For the Instructor]

You and your student might have to wait quite a while to complete all the lessons in Step Ten for obvious reasons – and it might not be practical or possible to attempt lessons in rainy conditions, given your local climate.

On the other hand, it is not necessary for her to master every facet of bad-weather driving before obtaining a license. Just do not recommend that the student drive in heavy rain or fog unless she has spent some time in those conditions under supervision. If the student has completed all of the other lessons, however, and if rain or fog is forecast, you can use it to your advantage.

Repeat (Mostly) Everything in Harsh Weather

When clouds gather, you should repeat Steps Three through Nine, in that order. Allow the student to become familiar with the aspects of rainy or foggy weather starting out in less intense conditions. Even such basics as using windshield wipers and washers and the defoggers should be practiced away from traffic at first. Everything the student has learned under fair skies should be repeated. Go back through the neighborhoods, the commercial strips, rural roads, city streets and highways, both uncrowded and crowded. Go back through as much of it as you can, day and night, using the guidelines for rain and fog.

First Rule: Lights On

[For the Student]

As mentioned in Step Eight, any time the skies darken, you should make sure your headlights are on or turn them on manually. Remember, it is just as important to be seen as to see. Your headlights make your vehicle much more visible, particularly at a distance.

Dealing with Fog

Fog usually does not change road conditions; it only limits visibility. That is still a potentially hazardous condition, but it is a simple one to deal with: Make your vehicle as visible as possible to everyone else, and slow down until your speed matches your CLEAR ZONE. Most fog-related accidents happen because drivers fail to match their speed to their ability to see.

In light fog and moderate fog, make sure your lights are on – low-beams only. Fog reflects high-beams with a lot of glare and actually reduces your vision. If your vehicle is equipped with fog lights, use them as well.

If you are traveling on a highway and fog forces you to slow down more than 10 kilometers an hour under the speed limit, turn your flashers on. They will alert traffic behind you that you are not traveling at normal speed.

Follow everything you have learned about creating a **CLEAR ZONE**. Slow down until your zone matches your speed. Do this even if it means slowing down to a crawl.

Be especially aware of what is going on behind you. Many drivers behave as carelessly in fog as in clear weather. They drive too fast for conditions. If you see headlights approaching from behind, make sure the vehicle is slowing down as it nears you. If not, activate your flashers. If that fails to work, pull over. Let them pass by. You are always better off behind a careless driver.

Rainy Days

You might think that rain does not change the rules of driving much. After all, it is only water, but there are several ways rain can make streets and roads more hazardous:

- It reduces your vision, mostly because of the rain itself, and partly because darkened skies make it more difficult to see distant objects or discern shapes and colors.
- It reduces friction on the roadway, so stopping distances become greater and you could skid on curves.
- In heavy amounts, rain creates the possibility of flash flooding, which can trap you in low-lying areas.

Always treat rain with respect. It will present you with new challenges and experiences. Even light rain can increase your stopping distance.

Grow Accustomed to the Wipers

Simple and silly as it might seem, looking through your windshield with your wipers on could take some acclimation. Some people find wipers a major distraction. You must train yourself to ignore them by concentrating your attention on the road ahead.

You also need to learn how often to use your wipers. Almost all vehicles now feature variable-interval wiper controls. Operating them too rapidly could start them screeching annoyingly across the glass. Too slowly and they will not clear off the rain fast enough to keep your vision clear. There is no ideal frequency for wipers. It depends on conditions. Whenever it begins to rain, unless it is a heavy downpour, use your windshield washer when you turn your wipers on. I mentioned earlier how materials are constantly accumulating on your windshield, so if you turn your wipers on to wipe off a few raindrops, chances are you will create smears across the glass. Clean the glass and the wiper blades with the washers at the beginning.

Use Your Climate Controls
Increased humidity associated with rain and fog can affect your vision from inside the vehicle. Differences in temperature between the air inside and outside cause tiny water droplets to condense on the inside of the windshield. As soon as you see this happening, turn on your vehicle's defogger. If the weather is warm or only moderately cold, you might need to use the air conditioner as well, because it dehumidifies the interior air. In colder weather, use the defogger with the heater.

Use your rear window defogger if necessary but remember to turn it off as soon as the window is clear. If the weather is cold, as it is in the mountainous areas, you might need to defrost the windshield and rear window before starting out.

Something else to remember: If you need to adjust temperature or airflow controls on the instrument panel, be careful. If you shift your attention from the road to the interior of the vehicle, you will be traveling blind for as long as it takes. Even a five-second diversion at 50 kilometers an hour means you will travel 75 meters without looking. Any time you fail to CLEAR THE WAY, you are asking for trouble. So, try to make necessary adjustments at stop lights or stop signs.

Rainy Nights
Night driving in the rain can be particularly challenging, because rain on the windshield scatters the light of oncoming headlights, irritating your eyes and making it difficult to see ahead. Rain also changes the reflective patterns of the roadway, so that the lanes might become poorly defined. You must be careful to maintain an effective CLEAR ZONE in front of you and to watch for "Ice Cream"—inconsistencies of contrast, reflection and movement. Adjust your speed to compensate for reduced vision and the increased stopping distance required by the wet pavement.

Truck Spray
As I mentioned earlier, whenever you encounter large trucks, watch out for their bow waves of air. When you encounter them in heavy rain, watch out particularly for their bow sprays. These are

heavy zones of water extending at an angle from both sides of the front of the trucks. They can block your vision temporarily even if your wipers are working at maximum speed.

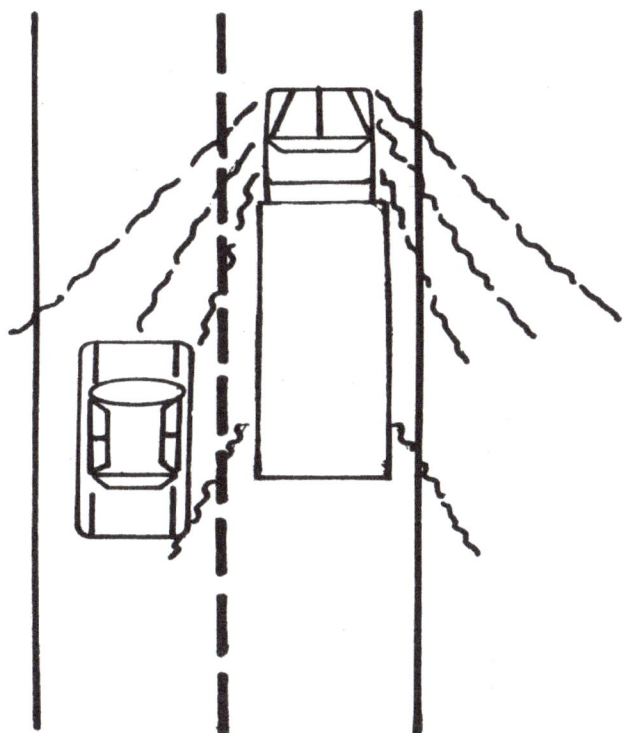

If a truck is about to pass you, or you are about to pass a truck, make sure you CLEAR THE WAY far ahead and know exactly which way the road is going, because your vision will be obscured for a few seconds. If you are being passed, ease off the gas for a moment until the truck's bow spray clears you. If you are passing, accelerate through it, but gently. Too much power on a saturated road could send you into a skid.

Water on the Roadway
When the road gets wet, the water acts as a lubricant. It reduces the ability of your tires to cling to the pavement. It increases stopping distance, and the road provides less friction to overcome your

vehicle's inertia going around curves. Too fast and you could slide, either off the road or into oncoming traffic.

This is true particularly during the first few minutes of a rainstorm, when water hitting the roadway mixes with oil and grime that have accumulated on the surface. Until the surface slick is washed away, the pavement can become slippery as ice.

When rain becomes heavy, and you are traveling at highway speeds, you could encounter a dangerous phenomenon called hydroplaning. Your vehicle's tires are designed with grooves in the tread. The grooves serve several purposes, one of which is to act as channels for water on the roadway. When they work properly, the tire tread grips the road and water is squeezed into the grooves.

In heavy rain, however, so much water accumulates on the pavement that the grooves cannot hold it all. When this happens, the tires lose contact. The vehicle actually begins to float on the water, and you lose steering and stopping control.

Another rain-related hazard: wet leaves on the roadway. They can be slippery and can send you into a skid if you encounter them on a curve or if you try to stop on them.

Perhaps the most hazardous condition of all is water flowing across a roadway – flash-flooding. In the United States, more people are killed by floods than any other weather-related cause. Many of them drown in vehicles, because they try to cross flooded roadways and are trapped or swept away by rising waters. Keep this in mind when you start out on a rainy day. Rain changes the rules. It narrows the limits of what you can do. You need to proceed carefully until you **LEARN THE LIMITS.**

Theme Five of Five: FEEL THE ROAD

How should you handle these conditions? The best way is to avoid them. That is easy in the case of flooding. Do not try to cross a flooded roadway. Even if you can see the pavement under a couple of centimeters of water, the flow could have undermined the roadbed. You could get stuck in a sinkhole. Do not risk it. Turn back and find an alternate route until the water level drops.

For other conditions, it is extremely important to know immediately if the tires are losing contact with the road. If it happens, and you do not notice, you easily could lose control. That means instead of driving down the road, you are suddenly riding inside a vehicle with a mind of its own. You could end up off the road, possibly upside down. Or, you could collide with something: a tree, a lamp post, a barrier or another vehicle.

You never want to be in this situation. The best way is to slow down in wet weather. That is good, but it might not always be enough. You must be able to detect loss of traction instantly. To do this, you have to **FEEL THE ROAD**.

As you drive, your brain is receiving various sensory inputs. Those inputs come from your hands on the steering wheel, your feet on the pedals, and your whole body sitting in the seat. In a way, you are connected to your vehicle, and it is connected to the road. From it, you sense direction, speed, acceleration and deceleration.

You also must learn to sense what the tires are doing. Several things can happen:
- You are driving in a straight line, but suddenly your drive wheels start spinning faster than they should, and perhaps your vehicle begins to "fish-tail" – its back end slipping from side to side.
- You are in a turn, but you begin to slide toward the outside of the curve.
- You have turned the steering wheel, but the vehicle continues to move straight ahead.
- You press the brake pedal, but the vehicle does not slow down, and it begins to swerve sideways.
- You try to start, but the wheels spin and the vehicle does not move.

In all but the last case, the results can be dangerous if you cannot restore traction immediately. The longer you go without reacting, the more likely you are to end up losing control. So you must learn to sense when the tires are beginning to slip. How? The best way is to practice, but you cannot go out into traffic and practice. You must start where your mistakes will not harm you or anyone else. You must go back to the parking lot.

Skidding Should Be Practiced

[For the Instructor]

Unless the student can experience skidding under supervision, and learn to anticipate it and control it, she will remain at a disadvantage. Skidding should be practiced, so that reacting to it becomes reflexive. If this has not happened before she obtains the license, you should recommend limits on her driving. She should not attempt high-speed highways in rainy weather, for example.

Basic Skid Exercises
There are three types of skids:
1. Stopping skids
2. Turning skids
3. Power skids

The first two can be practiced in the parking lot. The third is better experienced on the open road, but if the student becomes accustomed to the first two, and reads this section carefully, she should be able to react properly to the third if it occurs.

Wait for a heavy rain and return to the parking lot. Begin as you did in Step One, with basic movements. Before the student can learn to control a skid, she must learn what a skid feels like. So, start at one end of the lot, accelerate quickly, and stop hard at the other end. No steering, no control, simply hit the brakes and see what happens.

Try these free-style hard stops several times. Watch the student's reaction. Is she nervous? If so, continue the practice until things calm down. The objective is to condition her to the sensation of a possible skid and a sudden stop on wet pavement – including the sensation of the antilock brakes activating.

Antilock brakes require steady pressure. In older vehicles, standard brakes required a pumping motion for stopping on slick surfaces. ABS does the pumping for you. It is a technical advance meant to provide some control during a skid. But it creates a strange sensation, so it should be experienced and practiced to provide conditioning, and the empty parking lot forgives errors.

This exercise might need more than one session. Controlling a stopping skid requires reflexes, and they take a little time to develop. So spend a little time. Have the student work on it until she can do it consistently: Slam on the brakes, feel the skid, keep the vehicle in a straight line and bring it to a controlled stop.

'F.Re.S.H.'

[For the Student]

Skidding might seem like something you should fear, but if you follow the rules, you can avoid losing complete control of the vehicle.

Why do vehicles skid? When the road surface is slippery, the tires lose their ability to grip. When that happens, you can no longer control your direction or speed. Your vehicle might as well be on four soccer balls as four tires.

How do you overcome this? You must react in the right combination:
- Feel the skid beginning?
- Remove your foot from the gas or the brake.
- Steer to correct your Heading.

Remember:
Feel, Remove, Steer, Heading

"Head" is the critical element here. You want to keep yours, meaning stay cool and do not panic if you feel a skid. You should know well by now that the first thing to do in almost any situation like this is take your foot off the gas.

You also need to keep your head pointed in the direction you want to go. As I mentioned earlier, your hands will steer where you look. It is a little more complicated when you are trying to slow down, because you need to steer to correct your heading while exerting the right amount of pressure on the brakes. It will feel strange until you become accustomed to the sensation, but if you practice sufficiently you will never be caught off-guard.

Turning Skids

[For the Instructor]

There are two ways to practice turning skids: First, start out quickly with the wheels turned sharply. If the parking lot is wet enough, you should be able to skid on it. Second is to try a sharp turn at speed. In both situations, you want the student to correct for the skid. That should be easy when she is starting out. All that is needed is to ease off the gas and steer to straighten out.

The second skid is more difficult. At a high enough speed and a sharp enough turn, it is almost impossible to correct – but that is not a problem because you want the student to experience the situation. You want to condition her to avoid such a skid while on the road.

Make sure there is plenty of room and no one else is around when you try this.

Select a place in the lot with no obstructions or outside curbs, a place where the student can make a sharp turn without hitting anything. The ideal situation is a racetrack-like course with two turns and two straightaways.

Start out at least 15 meters from the first turn and have the student accelerate toward it. Have her try to hold the course through the turn without slowing down. The first try is likely to be messy, but you want the student to lose control.

Then start over. You want the student to accomplish three things here:
- Become conditioned to the feel of a skid
- Recover from it
- Sense the proper speed to turn on a slippery surface, so a skid can be avoided in the first place
-

This is serious business, but it also can be fun. In fact, it can be the most fun you will have during this process. Because it is fun, spend a lot of time with it. The more time the student spends skidding in the parking lot, the more able she will be to anticipate a skid on the road and recover from it. The key is repeated exposure under controlled conditions.

Power and Speed Are Enemies

[For the Student]

Sufficient rain can reduce or even eliminate the traction between the road surface and your tires. That is why, on wet roads, you might see vehicles spinning their wheels loudly but going nowhere. The road surface has become too slippery for the tires to grip. So the driver has difficulty controlling both momentum and direction.

Speed and power make things worse. The faster you go the more inertia the vehicle builds up. Because you need friction with the road to overcome inertia, and because water on the surface reduces friction, you will have less ability to overcome it. So, if you try to turn at too high a speed, inertia will overwhelm the traction of your tires, forcing you sideways.

In the case of acceleration, if you use too much power, your drive wheels will begin slipping and will throw you into a condition called a power skid. The tires on your drive wheels spin freely, causing loss of control. This is a particularly dangerous situation because it often happens at highway speeds.

The number one tool you have for driving safely on slippery roads is to lower your speed and to accelerate and decelerate gradually. Driving gently provides control. Driving aggressively loses control. It is that simple.

Test the Road

One of the most hazardous conditions on wet roads is the power skid. You could be driving along with complete traction, and then suddenly you find yourself spinning out of control.

Again, if you moderate your speed in wet conditions you should not have to worry about sudden skids. The best way to avoid this is to lower your speed, but another way is to test the road surface periodically. Once in a while, hit your brakes briefly and see what happens. Just for a second, push hard on the pedal and see how much you slide or if the ABS activates. If either happens, you will know to take it more slowly and carefully, and you will be less likely to be surprised by a sudden skid.

Make sure, however, that no other vehicles are around you when you try this, and do it only on a completely open and straight stretch of roadway.

One More Thing About Power Skids

Sometimes, though not often, taking your foot off the gas will not be enough to counter a skid. The minimum power still being delivered to the drive wheels might be enough to continue loss of control. In limited situations, you might need to shift into neutral to disconnect the power. Your best strategy is still to lower your speed, but if you misjudge remember to disconnect power to the wheels until you regain control.

Back on the Roads

[For the Instructor]

When the student begins to feel comfortable with skidding in the parking lot, head back to the streets, roads and highways. The object there is not to skid but to drive safely in bad weather. You want to work extensively on the proper speed for conditions. That is the best safe strategy. Then, if a skid does develop, the student should be able to recover from it by following the procedures you covered in the parking lot exercises.

The Biggest Danger

[For the Student]

Even if you learn everything in this section perfectly, you still could be in danger in harsh weather or dangerous roads – from other drivers. Many people who drive on slippery roads have little regard for such conditions, and many of them fail to exercise even the most basic caution.

Along with all else you have learned, remember to watch out for other drivers behaving unsafely. Your best defense is to stay away from anyone driving too fast or recklessly, or anyone who appears unable to cope with conditions. On slippery or foggy roads, incompetent drivers can be just as dangerous as aggressive ones.

TWO LAST ITEMS

[For the Student]

I would like to share two more bits of advice to you, one of them an overriding approach and the other an emergency maneuver I hope you will never need.

The approach involves something that has become a scourge among drivers the world over: distraction. This age of effortless wireless communication has proven a powerful attraction to people all over the world. In particular, personal devices are occupying more and more time, involving text messages and telephone conversations. One of the downsides of all this activity is unfortunately, an increase in injuries and deaths among motorists and pedestrians. People who should be paying attention to where they are going are glancing or staring at their screens.

As you complete your training and become a member of the driving population, please consider this phenomenon with great seriousness. Avoid the temptation, for example, to text while driving. Likewise, avoid reading texts while driving, and confine your phone conversations to times when you are stopped – not while moving along the highways. Please, protect yourself, your passengers and those around you – please keep your eyes on the road at all times.

The emergency maneuver is an elaboration of something I mentioned twice in the text. The first was how to interact with an oncoming vehicle on a street or road. The second was how to turn left safely behind an oncoming vehicle. Both are based on a principle that is also taught to American football players. It is called "run to daylight." It means that if you want to avoid tangling with another object, such as an opposing player who is determined to tackle you, the best method is to concentrate on where that player is not – on the empty space away from the would-be tackler.

As you might recall, when I advised how to pass by an oncoming vehicle, or turn left behind an oncoming vehicle, I advised concentrating on the empty space next to that vehicle. If you are ever involved in an emergency situation on the highway, try to remember that advice. Do not look directly at a vehicle approaching you or an object you are approaching. Concentrate instead on any empty space that might be available and steer toward it. Keep steering toward it until you are stopped. It could provide you with enough of a margin to avoid a collision.

I hope you never need it. But please try to remember it.

GO FORTH WITH PRIDE AND CONFIDENCE

[For the Student]

I hope you have found the advice and lessons in this book helpful, and I hope you will follow them as long as you drive. Please be assured, as I mentioned before, that this material if you practice it consistently will serve you well.

If I might, I would like to mention something to you that is different from anything I have written in my previous books about driving safety. You, the women of Saudi Arabia, will be joining women all over the world in enjoying the freedom that operating an automobile provides. And yes, unfortunately, you will also be sharing the frustration we all feel in dealing with traffic and aggression and that newest of roadway afflictions, distracted drivers.

But you will be unique among all nations. You will be the first group to be trained using only the latest technology (simulators) and, if you have learned using this book, the best advice gleaned from many years of experience on the roads. That means you have an opportunity to show the entire world what a population of properly trained and properly functioning motorists can now accomplish. Please recognize and take pride in that fact. Astonishing as it seems, during your lifetime you might drive nearly one million kilometers, something your ancestors could not have imagined.

I hope this is what will happen. I hope you will retain everything you have learned, take it seriously and strive to become exemplary in your performance behind the wheel. That you will obey the traffic laws, behave courteously and always exercise caution.

I likewise will take pride because I will have contributed a small part to your knowledge in this exciting new phase of your lives.

Last, I hope that as you gain experience and confidence on the road, you will consider teaching your daughters to drive well when they reach the appropriate age.

If so, I believe the world will look upon you with admiration and favor.

As-Salaam-Alaikum

Lesson Guide (a check-off list)

INTRODUCTION FOR THE STUDENT

- Getting Started ( )

INTRODUCTION FOR THE INSTRUCTOR

- An Approach to Teaching ( )
- The Best Place to Start ( )
- The First Day ( )
- The Pre-Drive Checklist ( )
- Gripping the Wheel ( )

TEN STEPS TO BASIC SKILLS

STEP ONE: Basic Moves

- Theme One of Five: CLEAR THE WAY (Student) ( )
- Clean and Clear (Student) ( )
- Patience, Patience (Student) ( )
- Positioning the Vehicle ( )
- Around and Around ( )
- Proper Steering (Student) ( )
- Keep It Slow ( )
- Backing Well (Student) ( )
- All Together ( )
- Practice 'Called Stops' ( )

STEP TWO: Quiet Streets, Back Roads

- Continue to Move Slowly (Student) ( )
- On Calm Streets ( )
- 'Live' Parking Drills ( )
- More Parking Practice (Student) ( )
- Stop Signs (Student) ( )
- First Encounters (Student) ( )
- Turnarounds ( )
- Turning Around in Tight Spaces (Student) ( )
- A Little Faster, A Little Busier ( )
- Learning to React (Student) ( )
- Dealing with Impatience ( )

STEP THREE: Busy But Slow Encounters

- Low-Speed Hazards (Student) ( )
- Do Not Assume Anything (Student) ( )
- Outside Then Inside ( )
- Parking Garage Alert (Student) ( )

STEP FOUR: Stop and Go

- Dealing with Traffic (Student) ( )
- Making a CLEAR ZONE (Student) ( )
- Do Not Violate Your Own CLEAR ZONE (Student) ( )
- Along the Strip ( )
- See a Stop Light? Drive Light (Student) ( )
- Watch Out for Red-Light Runners (Student) ( )
- Increase the Complexity ( )
- Roundabouts (Student) ( )

- Changing Lanes (Student) ( )
- Left Turns (Student) ( )
- Make All Turns with Caution ( )
- Look for the Empty Space (Student) ( )
- Avoid 'The Canyon' (Student) ( )
- Do Not Follow Large Vehicles Too Closely (Student) ( )
- Teach Navigation ( )
- A Special Note about Center Turn Lanes (Student) ( )

STEP FIVE: Countryside

- Driving Is Sensing (Student) ( )
- Take the Time ( )
- Looking Well Ahead (Student) ( )
- Check Your Speed (Student) ( )
- Handling Curves Correctly ( )
- Looking and Curving (Student) ( )
- Watch for Loss of Control ( )
- Theme Two of Five: LEARN THE LIMITS (Student) ( )
- Countryside Hazards ( )
- Countryside Cruising (Student) ( )
- Oncoming Traffic (Student) ( )
- Beware of Road Squeezes (Student) ( )
- Beware of Drop-Offs (Student) ( )
- Practicing a Drop-Off ( )
- Other Countryside Hazards (Student) ( )
- Theme Three of Five: SHARE THE ROAD (Student) ( )
- The Special Danger of Railroad Crossings (Student) ( )
- Beware of Tailgaters ( )
- Read the Road Signs (Student) ( )
- Getting Up to Speed (Student) ( )

STEP SIX: Getting Up to Highway Speeds

- Easing onto Highways ( )
- Merging ( )
- Clear the Ramp First (Student) ( )
- Exiting (Student) ( )
- Be Courteous to Merging and Exiting Vehicles (Student) ( )
- Keeping to the Right ( )
- Stay Right, Stay Safe (Student) ( )
- Four-Lane Passing (Student) ( )
- More About Blind Spots (Student) ( )
- Being Passed (Student) ( )
- Hold the Line (Student) ( )
- Do Not Take 80 Lightly (Student) ( )
- Emergency Stopping ( )
- Stopping Safely in an Emergency (Student) ( )
- Returning to the Road Safely (Student) ( )
- Two-Lane Roads ( )
- You Will Need Two Sets of Eyes ( )
- Enter With Caution (Student) ( )
- Highway Turnoffs (Student) ( )
- Other Highway Encounters (Student) ( )
- Two-Lane Passing (Student) ( )

STEP SEVEN: Night Driving

- Lights On (Student) ( )
- Low-Beams (Student) ( )
- High-Beams (Student) ( )
- Headlight Limits (Student) ( )
- 'Ice Cream' (Student) ( )

STEP EIGHT: City Streets

- Steady, Straight and Calm (Student) ( )
- Theme Four of Five: THINK AHEAD (Student) ( )
- Parallel Parking (Student) ( )
- Practice Makes Perfect ( )

STEP NINE: Into Heavy Traffic

- Heavy-Traffic Skills ( )
- Approaching Heavy Traffic (Student) ( )
- Going Against the Crowd (Student) ( )
- Relativity Is the Key (Student) ( )
- Always Be Predictable (Student) ( )
- The Safest Place (Student) ( )
- Stay Out of the Left Lane (Student) ( )
- Tight Merges (Student) ( )
- Mixing Loops (Student) ( )
- Blending (Student) ( )
- Clogs (Student) ( )
- Do Not Pass on the Right (Student) ( )
- Watch Out for Weavers and Slicers (Student) ( )
- Better Behind Than Ahead (Student) ( )
- Holding Your Line (Student) ( )
- Navigating Narrow Lanes (Student) ( )

STEP TEN: Harsh Weather

- Repeat (Mostly) Everything in Harsh Weather ( )
- First Rule: Lights On (Student) ( )
- Dealing With Fog (Student) ( )
- Rainy Days (Student) ( )

- Grow Accustomed to the Wipers (Student) ( )
- Use Your Climate Controls (Student) ( )
- Rainy Nights (Student) ( )
- Truck Spray (Student) ( )
- Water on the Roadway (Student) ( )
- Theme Five of Five: FEEL THE ROAD (Student) ( )
- Skidding Should Be Practiced ( )
- Basic Skid Exercises ( )
- 'F.Re.S.H.' (Student) ( )
- Turning Skids ( )
- Power and Speed Are Enemies ( )
- Test the Road ( )
- One More Thing About Power Skids (Student) ( )
- Back on the Roads ( )
- The Biggest Danger (Student) ( )

LESSON LOG

LESSON LOG

LESSON LOG

LESSON LOG

LESSON LOG

LESSON LOG

LESSON LOG

www.ingramcontent.com/pod-product-compliance
Lightning Source LLC
Chambersburg PA
CBHW041536220426
43663CB00002B/51